WALK BY
FAITH

John + Karen

God Bless!

David Kline

D A V I D   K L I N E

ISBN 978-1-63525-302-3 (Paperback)
ISBN 978-1-63525-304-7 (Hard Cover)
ISBN 978-1-63525-303-0 (Digital)

Christian Faith Publishing, Inc.
296 Chestnut Street
Meadville, PA 16335
www.christianfaithpublishing.com

Printed in the United States of America

DEDICATION

Thank you, Mom,
for pushing me to put my story onto paper.

FOREWORD

A life-altering injury can either diminish a person's character, or become the platform from which true character grows. That describes David Kline perfectly: enthusiastic... optimistic... a go-getter... and a man whose passion is to showcase the glory of God. In *Walk by Faith*, you will discover a man who looks at every challenge as a wonderful opportunity – and after reading his story, you'll do the same!

– Joni Eareckson Tada,
Joni and Friends International Disability Center.

PROLOGUE

I t was quiet, oddly quiet, there under the water. And very still. *Well, God will heal me.* That was my first thought. Somehow I already knew that I had just broken my neck. Yet at that very moment, I did not know just how drastic and life-changing that moment would be.

CHAPTER 1

Like most people I know, I was born at a very young age (that's the joke I like to make). On October 30, 1969, I was born in the usual way, and I was a healthy baby with no disability. We can't pick our parents, so I guess I got lucky. My father, Jack Toney, 22, had graduated with honors at the Air Force Academy in Colorado Springs. As one of the top cadets, he accepted the opportunity to earn his MBA at UCLA before starting pilot training. At the time, my mother, Linda Wilks, 20, was living in Westwood, California, near UCLA. One summer day, three U.S. Air Force cadets moved into her apartment building. She got one look at my dad in his swimming trunks by the pool and was in love. His Southern drawl didn't hurt either. Four months later, they were engaged, and two months after that, they were married. I was born two and a half years later.

My birth name was Virgil Jackson Toney III. Obviously, I was named after my birth father and his father. It is rumored that the Jackson name descends to me from one of the most gifted tactical commanders in U.S. history, General Stonewall Jackson. Virgil Jackson Toney III is quite a mouthful, and it's hard to imagine calling a baby by that name, so I was given the nickname Tripper. I just recently found out that *Tripper* was short for *triple*, because I was the third generation to carry the name. So I was known as Tripper Toney. I guess that name is a little catchier than the original.

I was born in the Panama Canal Zone. My father was stationed at an American Air Force base (Albrook) at the time. I have no memory of this. As far as I know, my parents could be making up my birth story. But I'm gonna believe they're telling the truth. Besides, I've seen a baby picture of me in a jungle with an iguana. We moved to Sacramento a year and a half later. My parents divorced shortly afterward. After the divorce, my dad was not much a part of my life. I would stay with him and his new wife for a week every summer and every other Christmas. Despite the limited contact, I have always liked him and have always thought he was a good guy and a man of integrity. I have never asked him why he and my mom divorced.

My mom and I moved into a small apartment in Santa Barbara, California. A couple years later, we met Richard Kline, a handsome and charming restaurant owner who was four years younger than my mother. He and my mom began dating. Less than six months later, when I was five years old, the two got married. This was just fine with me! I thought he was great! He taught me how to play sports, how to make people laugh, and how to tie my shoes. I didn't call him Richard. I called him *Dad*.

Two other great things happened to me at this young age. First of all, I became a lifelong fan of the Dallas Cowboys. Not only did the team and coach have class, but they also had great talent and a winning record (not that I understood that at such a young age; I just liked cowboys and

the color blue). The second thing, infinitely more import-
ant (I'm sure the Cowboys would agree), is that I became a
Christian. This is the best decision I have made and will ever
make in my life. I don't remember making the decision, but
I know that it happened. I am so glad and so fortunate that
God grabbed hold of me at such a young age!

One week after my sixth birthday, I got a new brother.
We were expecting a girl, so my parents had already wall-
papered his bedroom in a soft yellow. But instead of a girl,
Jonathan was a boy, and I was happy to have a younger
brother. I remember lovingly holding him up in my arms,
only to have him throw up in my face. That was a bonding
moment for sure!

Now with two boys in the family, my dad added the
phrase "and sons" to the name of his restaurant. This
change and, no doubt, the fact that there was a new member in our family, prompted me to make a change myself.
I noticed that my dad's last name was Kline, my mom's
last name was Kline, and Jonathan's last name was Kline,
but I had a different last name. I wanted to be a Kline too.
So I decided I would change my name. Yes, at six years
old, I decided I would change my name—not just my last
name, but my first and middle names as well. The name
Tripper had never bothered me; I never got teased (believe
it or not). I just wanted a new name. I liked my best friend
David's name, so I picked *David* to be my new name.

I was very serious about this. My mom discovered this
right away. "Tripper?" she called to me from the kitchen.
There was no answer. "Tripper!" Still no answer. So she
walked to my room, saw me playing there, and asked,
"Why didn't you answer me?"

I replied, "My name isn't *Tripper* anymore. I changed it to *David.*"

"Oh," she said. Not realizing I was serious, she played along and said, "Well, then, you'll need a middle name too." She got out her baby book of names and said, "Pick a name you like."

I opened up the book to the first page and picked the very first name listed there: *Aaron.* "I'll take it," I said. So I became David Aaron Kline. I wouldn't answer to anything else, so my family, friends, and school all accepted my new name.

My biological father, Jack Toney, wasn't thrilled with my name change, which was understandable. I called him on the phone to tell him my exciting news. He immediately responded, "Put your mother on the phone." He eventually got over it, but he and my relatives on that side of the family still like to call me *Tripp* to this day, which is fine with me.

To actually change my name at six years old, I must have had a streak of independence and confidence, even at that young age. Another example occurred one summer day when a kid and I were throwing rocks across our quiet street. He wasn't really a friend, just a kid from my neighborhood. As a VW Bug drove by, my "friend" threw a rock at the car and hit it. The driver slammed on the breaks and turned around. The kid took off running, so I did too. As we were running away, I thought, *Wait a minute! I didn't hit the car. I didn't do anything wrong. I don't have to hide with this kid.* So I stopped in my tracks and went back. The driver found me. "I didn't throw the rock," I told the angry driver, so he took off after the other kid.

Six was quite a year for me, because not only did I have a brand-new baby brother and get to change my name, but I also discovered girls! I really liked girls! For a sheltered little boy, I somehow had figured out what I thought were "cool" moves. For example, whenever a little classmate melted my heart, I gave her whatever money I had in my pocket. I have no idea where I got this idea, but if this habit had continued throughout my lifetime, I would have gone broke long ago.

I had other six-year-old "moves" too. One afternoon, my classmate Lynn came over for a visit. While in my room, we decided to play "house". I pretended to be the dad, and I went off to work. While at work, I wrote "kiss longer" on a piece of paper and then put the paper in my briefcase. When I got home, my "wife" asked, "How was your day?" I then opened the briefcase and handed her the paper. I know I sound real smooth, but I don't think we even kissed.

Even though I really liked girls and had these supercool "moves," I just wasn't smart enough to figure everything out. For example, at school when we would play freeze tag at recess, none of the girls ever tagged me; I was too fast. I didn't figure out until much later that I shouldn't have tried to outrun the girls; I should've slowed down and let them tag me. Duh.

On a more serious note, I did learn three extremely valuable life lessons during this time in my life. The first occurred one day when my mom had done something to upset me. I don't even remember what it was, but I was so mad that I took out my pocket knife (no, this story is not about to take a dark turn), and I cut up the sheets on my bed. When I was finished, I looked at what I had done. Then I thought, *Now I have holes in my sheets. That was dumb.* At that young age, I learned that my actions have consequences and that I better really think things through before I act. I have never forgotten that lesson.

The second lesson happened when my mom and I had gone grocery shopping one day. After the grocery bags were packed in the trunk of our car, my mom and I got in the front seats. Out of the corner of her eye, she noticed a few lumps under my overalls on my chest. She reached in and pulled out the six rolls of Lifesavers I had stolen. My mom immediately marched me back into the store and found the manager. She made me confess to him what I had done. I felt such guilt and embarrassment that I never stole a thing again.

The third valuable life lesson I learned at that young age occurred at school. I had a big homework assignment due that day, but I had forgotten it at home. My teacher let me call my mom at home to have her bring my assignment to school for me. I asked my mom in my sweet, little voice, and she replied, "No." That was a shock, but it made such an impression on me that I have remembered every assignment since.

My dad Richard had set a goal for himself to be a millionaire by the time he reached the age of thirty. He was well on his way. He owned a successful restaurant. We lived just outside of Santa Barbara in Montecito, an extremely exclusive and wealthy community. Our house had a miniature soccer field and a paved basketball area. I even had a pony (that sounds so snotty). However, when my dad opened up a very large second restaurant, it failed. Soon, the business went bankrupt. We lost the second restaurant and had to sell our house and move to a small rental in downtown Santa Barbara. I was eight years old at this point. There were five of us now, including my new baby brother, Adam.

I never noticed the financial decline. To me, it just seemed like my parents wanted to move to a different house; I didn't know about bankruptcy. I was still fortunate enough to grow up in a Christian family with loving parents. I attended a good Christian school, went to church, and participated in all the family activities. We were a nice, happy family. That's all that mattered.

I don't think our bankruptcy was the reason I started to collect aluminum cans. I was an eight-year-old boy, so of course, I wanted to buy football cards and *Star Wars* cards. Even if our family still had money, my parents would not have just bought me everything I wanted. If I wanted kid stuff, I had to earn it.

So my friend and I would grab plastic trash bags, jump on our bikes, and head off to the nearby shopping centers. We'd go behind the businesses and into the alleys searching for the big trash dumpsters. One of us would climb up and jump into the dumpster, dig through the garbage looking for aluminum cans, and then throw them out onto the ground. The other would smash the cans flat with the heel of his foot. Then we'd throw the cans in our bags and go searching for the next "gold mine." Once our bags were full of flattened cans, we'd take them to the recycling center for cash. Can you believe that my parents had no problem with me digging through city dumpsters? I guess it was a different time back then. In fact, at eight years old, I had to ride the city bus by myself to get to school, transferring busses twice. That sounds crazy nowadays.

It was a different time, but for me, it was a normal time as well. I was just your typical kid, living a typical life. That would completely change.

Those are some good looking parents!

My father Jack throwing me into the Grand Canyon. ☺

My mom and I are ready for trick-or-treating!

Lookin' sharp for Easter! (1976)

My dad Richard, Jonathan, Trigger, and I
in our backyard in Montecito.

CHAPTER 2

Shortly after my tenth birthday, we left Santa Barbara and moved north to the Gold Country in Grass Valley, California. Many years later, I learned the reasons for our move. My parents didn't want to raise us in Santa Barbara because of the obsession of wealth held by so many. In addition, they were hoping that a change in scenery might be good for their marriage. Of course, I was sad to move away from my town and my friends, but by no means was I devastated. Not only was our new house big and beautiful, but I soon discovered that my neighborhood was filled with boys my age! I had no trouble making new friends and feeling at home in my new hometown, a location set among majestic pines and gold mines.

At my new Christian school, my athletic gifts became evident as I excelled in soccer, basketball, and track, often winning the MVP awards. I also competed academically, sang in the school choir, and performed in community theater. And possibly more exciting than those accomplishments, girls were starting to notice me. It felt like I was becoming a confident young man. Life was good, very good!

My family and home life were such blessings growing up. Having a loving family was definitely part of it. I never heard yelling in the house. No one swore or put down another family member. In fact, I was always so cautious to not say something to my little brothers that might harm their young egos. Weird, huh? What older brother does that? The worst thing I ever did to my brothers was when I put underwear on Jon's head and called him *Underwear Man*.

I always knew that my parents loved me and would be there for me. I knew that my mom would be there when I got home from school and that my dad would be home shortly thereafter. I knew that if I wanted to play catch or shoot hoops with my dad, he would always say yes. I knew that we would always eat dinner together at six o'clock. I knew that we would always go to church together on Sunday and that my dad would read the Bible and pray with me every night. Such routine and security was stability. A stable life like that is both critical and comforting for a kid—for anyone.

It was at this age when, out of the blue, I wondered if I really had become a Christian when I was five years old. For all those years, I thought I had. *What if I didn't?* I wondered. *I better do it again, just in case.* So I prayed, right there in my front yard, "Dear God, just in case I didn't actually do this years ago, I'm going to do it now. Thank you for loving me so much that Your Son, Jesus, died on the Cross for my sins. I know that Jesus rose from the grave, and I ask that He will live in my heart so that I may go to heaven. Please forgive me of all of my sins and please give me strength each day to live for You. Thank you, God." *Ahhhh.* I felt better after that. It was good to know that I had for sure taken care of such an important decision as my eternal destination and my peace and joy on this earth.

Over the next few years, athletics became a major part of my life for a number of reasons. First of all, they were so much fun. Second, I was very good at them. Third, they were a great way to exercise and stay in good shape. And fourth, my teams almost always won. For example, with soccer, I began playing when I was five years old. I played on eleven teams in the years that followed. Ten of those teams placed first in their leagues. My basketball teams and track teams also placed first. Winning numerous events at track meets allowed me to compete in the Junior Olympic trials. Winning is nice.

Soccer was definitely my favorite sport. I loved it. I loved the speed, the maneuvers, and the emotion. I had good ball control, a strong shot, quick speed, and great endurance. Walking out onto the field for practice after school, my cleats hanging over my shoulder, the warm summer air, the confidence in my ability—all set the scene for a good afternoon. I was in my element. I was even intoxicated by the smell of fresh-cut grass.

As a freshman and sophomore in high school, I played on the varsity team. I set school records and won numerous Most Valuable Player awards, Most Inspirational awards, league awards, and a Coach's Award. When I was fifteen, I travelled to England with a team of players from throughout California to compete with international youth teams in the Ipswich Cup. Back in the United States, I received offers to play soccer for two private colleges. My purpose here is not to boast, but to establish that life was good, I was accustomed to success, and things were going my way.

One of my main strengths in soccer was that I could run forever. As an example, during timed runs at practice, I would be way ahead of my teammates. My coach, Thad Kopec, would comment as I ran by, "How do you keep such a steady, fast pace?"

"I'm singing the song 'Mr. Roboto' in my head and running to the beat," I yelled back.

Coach would say that I could "run like the wind."

I could just keep going and going and going. Most mornings, I jogged my usual three-mile loop through the Empire Mine State Park. The eight hundred acres of the park contained the grounds and remnants of California's most productive gold mine, and it was right across the street from my house! I knew those woods well, for I had played in them since fifth grade. By seventh grade, I jogged those trails for exercise before school. Sounds crazy, right?

I remember running alone one morning, and by the end of my loop, I didn't feel like stopping. I had a burst of energy and drive, so I just kept running. Up hills, down hills, I ran through parts of that forested park I had never seen. It was a blast! On another morning, I remember running alongside a remote road that circled the park as a pickup truck drove past, stopped, and then backed up. It was still fairly dark, and there was a slight drizzle. The driver rolled down his window and called out, "Boy, are you okay? Is somethin' the matter?"

"I'm fine. I'm just joggin'. Thanks," I replied as I kept on running.

I was pretty determined and disciplined in my jogging. I wanted to be in great shape and be a great athlete, so

I jogged every day. When I wanted to accomplish something, I always worked hard to get it. I applied this to all areas of my life. When I wanted a stereo, I got a paper route to earn the money to buy it. I don't know if my work ethic was innate or taught to me, but I have always been glad I had it. Maybe I learned it from my favorite book as a child—*The Little Engine That Could*.

For a similar reason, as a teen, I was inspired by the movie *Chariots of Fire*. I even learned to play the theme song on the piano. The movie is based on the true story of two runners in the 1924 Olympics, Eric Liddell, a devout Scottish Christian who runs for the glory of God, and Harold Abrahams, an English Jew who runs to overcome prejudice.

One of my all-time favorite movie quotes is in this movie. In a discussion with his sister about the ethics of running on Sunday, Liddell justifies his controversial decision to run by saying, "I believe God made me for a purpose, but He also made me fast. And when I run, I feel His pleasure." That quote always resonated with me. I believed God made me for a purpose. I sometimes wondered and even hoped and dreamed that He would use my athletic ability to serve Him. That would've been awesome!

During my early high school years, life was not completely perfect for me though. When I was fifteen, one day, my mom suddenly moved out, and my parents' hidden marital problems were exposed. This was a shock! My brothers and I had no idea our parents were having problems. They had done a very good job of shielding us kids from their arguments. My brothers were devastated. For me, it was very sad. It was a crack in my ideal childhood and in my stable life. While I hoped things would get better, this was a very confusing and difficult time for Jonathan and Adam. After a few weeks, our parents must have arrived at some sort of reconciliation, for my mom moved back home.

Unfortunately, this reconciliation did not last long. My mom moved out again, but this time she got her own apartment. This definitely felt serious. Though my brothers and I still saw her often, it was difficult to not find her at home after school and not there living in our home. It was so strange not having one family in one house but having to go to two houses in order to see each parent. We no longer went to church together as one family. In fact, I often had to go by myself. My "perfect" family life had changed so much.

A year later, my parents were still separated. My mom bought her own house twenty minutes away. My parents' separation was frustrating for me on a number of levels. Of course, I wanted our family back together. Another issue was that I was sixteen years old and was focused on school, work, sports, friends, and girls. I didn't have the time or energy to be going back and forth to two houses very often. Over time, I began to get used to the separation and not seeing my mom as often as I had been accustomed.

After numerous attempts to patch up their marriage, my parents divorced a short time later. Thankfully, and to the credit of my parents, they each still supported me to the fullest in my academics and athletics. There was one positive aspect of my parents' divorce—at least in my mind. When my dad eventually got a girlfriend, he would often spend the weekend at her house. That meant I had the house to myself! What more could a teenager ask for?

For my remaining two years of high school, I decided to transfer from my Christian school to the local public high school. I transferred because my closest friends and a potentially better soccer team were at the public school. Though I went from a school of seventy students to a school of more than 2,800, I had no trouble making friends and enjoying my new surroundings. I had so much fun seeing my best friends every day! It didn't take long before I decided that my junior year of high school was my best year yet. I had a whole lot of friends, an excellent season in soccer, and the entire house to myself (some of the time). I was having the best time of my life.

I had a big group of great friends. Scott was one of my best friends. He was 6'7" and hilarious. Erik was also a very close friend. He was very creative and funny. Other good friends were Steve, Dave, Dane, Darren, Dan, and Lindsey. Some of us had been close for six years. The group consisted mostly of guys, but a few girls would usually hang out with us too.

Just about every weekend, I would have a party at my house. We would stay up until the early morning hours playing silly games that we made up, or we would go and run around in the Empire Mine State Park. Our favorite thing to do though was to make videos. We recorded many lip-syncing videos to popular rock songs by artists like Billy Idol, the Rolling Stones, and Quiet Riot. We also filmed a lot of impromptu skits and scenes that were very funny, like cowboys in a saloon, scenes in spaceships, exploding toilets, and bullet catching. We laughed nonstop! I have always thought we were the funniest group of guys I have ever known. We also were a very creative group, and if we thought of an idea, we'd do it. We were never bored. I had so much fun doing our silly and crazy activities!

We even started our own club, and we would meet every week before school for breakfast and plan out whose house we would teepee that weekend. Our targets were always friends of ours who never seemed to mind having their trees covered in toilet paper. I have to admit that we also teepeed the mayor's house; his daughter was one of our friends. We got caught and ran away. We also tee-peed our old school, Forest Lake Christian School. Halfway through the "job," all the campus lights went out, and as we fled the scene across the soccer field, the sprinklers came on and blasted us. We knew we had been busted. It turned out though that no one had seen us; the power had coin-cidentally gone off and then back on while we were up to our mischief.

We had another great prank planned for Forest Lake Christian School. This may sound hard to believe, but we honestly did still love our old school; this was just our way of showing our appreciation for educating us so well in our early years. The school was located just down the street from Lake of the Pines, a private, gated community with a man-made lake surrounded by over a thousand homes. Every year, the school would rent the clubhouse at the lake and have an end-of-the-year party there.

It was at the previous year's party that my friends and I planned a huge surprise for the school administration and other students. The entire area was gated, with only one entrance. At the entrance was a guard in a guardhouse and a very long sign that read "Lake of the Pines". My friends and I planned on sneaking up to the entrance the night before our school party and rearranging the giant wooden letters in the word *Lake* and the vowels in the word *Pines*. That's right, when we were finished, the sign would read "Leak of the Penis". Unfortunately, in our reconnaissance, we noticed that the guard at the gate was too alert and the letters were bolted on much too tight, so we were unable to accomplish our devious mission. Teenagers! So clever! That though is about as naughty as we got. I still think it was a great idea though.

My close friends and I also organized big events for all our friends from high school. We had New Year's Eve parties where we'd light dry dog food on fire and throw it in the air. We had Fourth of July parties where we'd blow stuff up. We had Christmas parties—no, it had nothing to do with explosives or fire—we simply exchanged gifts.

Our biggest event of the year though was Capture the Flag at Erik's house. Imagine five acres of fields, hills, forests, and creeks with rope swings, a barbeque, and a horseshoe pit. He and I would send out thirty to forty invitations to our friends, and without fail, almost all the guys would show up. As usual, some girls would hang out, help with food, and nurse our injuries.

When the event started at 5 p.m., Erik and I would be dressed in full camouflage and boots. I would greet each "participant" at the entrance to Erik's long driveway with a clipboard and checklist. Using walkie-talkies, I would inform Erik of arrivals, and then he would direct the parking at his house. We took our Capture the Flag seriously. From 5 to 9 p.m., we barbequed, played horseshoes, and hung out. From 9 to 11, we watched a movie like *First Blood*, starring Sylvester Stallone. From eleven to midnight, we prepared ourselves in camo clothes and camo face paint. Capture the Flag lasted from midnight to seven in the morning, followed by breakfast. What an awesome time! I didn't know any other high schoolers then and I don't know if any high schoolers today would, on their own, ever take the time to organize and run such a huge event.

All this craziness stayed fun because we shared the same morals and values. The peer pressure to drink or take drugs was never an issue. It is hard to believe in this day and age, but my friends and I did all those silly things without drugs or alcohol. In fact, we often would go to the store and buy Strawberry Daiquiri mix, but we would make the drinks virgin. It's true. What a bunch of squares!

Actually, I say that with pride. I'm so glad we avoided the stupid decisions people make while drunk. I didn't know any other teenagers who were as funny, creative, active, and innocent as our group. We never got into trouble. We were having too much fun! Good, quality friends are so important at that age. I believe, typically, a person will adopt the habits and traits of his/her friends; they will either bring you up or bring you down. My friends and I brought each other up. My friends were great.

With all these activities, friends, and fun, my faith in God was the most important thing to me. I had been a Christian for most of my life. My family had gone to church at least twice a week. We had prayed together before each meal. My brothers and I had attended Christian school and went to Christian camps every summer. I still read my Bible and prayed every night. I attended a weekly Bible study with my friends Steve, Dane, and Erik before school. Most of my choices were primarily based on what God says to do in His Word. I didn't drink or do drugs, because the Bible says to stay sober. I didn't have sex, because the Bible says sex was created for marriage. I didn't swear, because the Bible says to have speech that is pure. I really tried to live a godly life. And it wasn't hard either. I just set my mind to it and decided early on that those were things I would not do. And not once was I pressured to drink, do drugs, or have sex.

Even though no one ever tried to pressure me into doing something, there were though some people who, for fun, tried to get me to swear, because they had heard that I didn't, and so they wanted to hear something foul come out of my mouth. They were not successful.

My first car was a 1967 Camaro. Very cool. And very fast—though it would shake at 60 mph. My dad agreed to pay for half of the cost of my first car if I kept my grades up. I did. We bought this maroon Camaro for $1,200. It was a stick shift, and my dad said it was a bad stick shift too. I had learned to drive on automatics, and it took me a long time to learn how to drive this old Camaro. After struggling to figure out how to drive a bad stick shift, I was soon cruising around town in that car listening to U2, Tears for Fears, Oingo Boingo, and Depeche Mode.

Sadly, within six months, my Camaro died in the late afternoon on Highway 49; it just stopped running. I coasted off the highway and onto a small road about fifteen minutes outside of town. I had just enough coasting to get me to the parking lot of the Dew Drop Inn, a sketchy bar at the time. Without any other choice but to go inside to use the phone, I, a squeaky-clean, square, preppie kid in plaid shorts and Sperry Topsiders, entered a biker bar. The bartender was very kind and let me use the phone. While waiting for my dad to come pick me up, a scruffy biker dressed in black leathers started a very cordial conversation with me. "What brings you in here?" he asked.

"My car just died on the highway. I coasted down the hill. It's parked outside."

"I have a friend who lives down the street. You can keep your car there, if you like," he offered.

"Is he nice?" I asked.

"Well, he rides a Harley!" he eagerly replied. I guess, in a biker bar, "riding a Harley" equates to niceness. I politely thanked him, but my dad and I decided to have my car towed to a mechanic. For my first experience with bikers, they were very friendly.

After the mechanic diagnosed my Camaro as "dead," my dad and I drove (in his car) an hour to Sacramento to buy a new car for me. We found a used car, but it was new to me. We bought a 1976 BMW 2002. Very cool. It was light blue with a sun roof. Just my style.

Driving home, we stopped at Taco Bell to grab a bite to eat. The girl who took our order was very cute—long black hair, big brown eyes, and a great smile. As my dad and I were leaving, I said to him, "Just a sec. I'll be right back." I walked back to the counter, up to this beauty, and said, "Hi, my name is David. Can I take you out to dinner some time?"

"Yes," she said with a smile. "And, oh, my name is Maria."

We exchanged phone numbers and planned when to meet for our date. Over the next few months, I drove down to Sacramento a few times to take her out. Each time, my dad would make the same sarcastic joke about my date from Taco Bell, like, "Are you going to see the Taco Queen tonight?"

I spontaneously asked a lot of girls out like that. If I saw a pretty girl, I'd introduce myself and ask her out. I went out on a lot of dates. I was a good boy though. I had decided long before that I would wait for sex until marriage, and I was sticking to it. I kissed very few of my dates. I tried to be both respectful and respectable.

I did not have any long relationships though, the longest lasting only three months. It was my fault that my relationships didn't last long. Looking back, I now can admit that I had a "disease." My "disease" was that once a girl liked me, I stopped being interested in her. How sad. I left some really great girls because I was stupid.

One of the great girls I knew was Shelley Brooks, a very cute, smart, and funny girl I met when I was about twelve and she was thirteen. Our families became great friends through church, and we spent a lot of time together. Shelley and I could be total goofballs together. I really had a good time hanging out with her. It didn't take long before my mom and others would say to me, "Oooh, Shelley's in love with you! You two are going to get married some day!" Well, hearing that just made my "disease" kick in, and I didn't think of her in a romantic way and did not pursue a relationship with her. We would still hang out a lot, but I only thought of her as a friend. My interests were in other girls.

Shelley and I went to different schools and had different schedules of work, friends, and family, so we didn't see each other much during our first couple of years of high school. It was not until later in my junior year that we started to hang out again; my dad began to invite her parents over after a couple of years of infrequency. Shelley and I joked and laughed without missing a beat, as if no time had passed. One night, after dinner, my brothers, Shelley, and I were upstairs wrestling. I had her pinned. She was on her back, and I was holding her down, looking at her. *Wow, she's pretty!* I thought to myself. *And what a great girl!*

After wasting years catering to my ego and foolishness and not dating this terrific girl, I finally started to see the light. It was not long after this that I asked her out to dinner. She said yes. We made plans for Friday night, July 10.

Two weeks before our date, I attended a soccer camp in Santa Barbara. It was the prestigious Vogelsinger Academy, acclaimed for its international instructors and coaches. Many of the soccer students arrived from around the world. With such high-quality instruction and challenge, my skill level skyrocketed in just one week! Because of this instruction and training, I knew that I would be a much better player in the upcoming season. Opposing teams, watch out!

I originally hadn't planned to attend the Vogelsinger soccer camp. Instead, I had planned to travel with my high school choir to Europe, which was scheduled for the following week. As the choir trip approached, I decided it was just too much money and the soccer camp would be more beneficial for my athletic skills and my future. That decision changed my life.

With my junior year of high school completed, my senior year of high school was already beginning to shape up nicely. I was voted captain of the varsity soccer team for the fall season and also had been elected as the senior class vice president (my best friend, Erik, was elected president). I also qualified to sing in the best choir at my school. I had dreams and career plans to someday start my own business, start a band, or play professional soccer (or a combination of all three). In fact, a friend and I were writing songs together, and I felt confident that I would be playing soccer at the college level.

Looking back on my childhood, I personally think it was great. I honestly had success in just about anything I attempted. In school, I always made honor roll without having to study very much. I competed in math, spelling, and speech competitions. I was elected to class offices whenever I ran. I got the parts in school plays whenever I auditioned. It was no different with sports. I received Most Valuable Player awards, Coach's awards, and Most Inspirational awards. I competed successfully in three different sports. In the eleven different soccer seasons I played, I was always on a winning team.

I didn't know rejection—from friends, family, or girls. Success just happened. I wasn't lazy or a jerk. I worked hard and was a nice guy, but clearly I had a blessed and unusual childhood.

Things were certainly going my way. But things don't always go according to plan. The stability and success of my childhood are two things I lost in an instant and have not experienced very much since I was seventeen.

My life was about to take a sharp turn.

Mom congratulating me after a successful track meet.

8th grade athletic awards, but you're focusing on the short shorts.

My 9ᵗʰ grade year at Forest Lake, playing soccer on the varsity team.

Yes, that's dorky hair in my soccer photo for Nevada Union. (1986)

Adam, Aunt Cheryl, Uncle Norm, Nana, Jonathan,
Mom, and I on Mother's Day. (1987)

Scott and I. No, that's not a mullet; that's his hand.

Erik and I at Grad Night at Disneyland. We
got to go with the senior class.

Mom, Adam, and I a week before my accident.

Chapter 3

Tuesday, July 7, 1987 was forecasted to be a typical hot summer day in northern California. The morning was already warming up. I had been home from soccer camp for a few days and was excited for my high school's soccer tryouts at the end of the month. Since I had already been chosen to be the team captain, I wasn't worried about making the cut. My date with Shelley was Friday, and to make sure everything was perfect, I had made our dinner reservations at Friar Tuck's restaurant days ago. The week ahead promised good things were coming my way!

How could I, or anyone else in my life, expect that by the end of this beautiful summer day, all my dreams would come crashing down? Waking up that lazy, carefree morning, I had no idea that my life was about to change forever.

My mom planned to enroll at California State University, Sacramento, studying for her psychology degree, so she asked me to babysit Jonathan (11) and Adam (9) and the two young daughters of Donna, my mom's longtime friend. It was a hot July afternoon, so the kids and I planned to go swimming at the lake. Before my mom left for Sacramento, she handed me a picnic basket with our lunch, promising on her return to bring fixings for a barbeque dinner to celebrate the new chapter in her life.

As the kids and I left the house, Donna took me aside and asked me to keep a close eye on her girls. "Of course!" I replied. What I didn't know was what prompted Donna to say that. Apparently, the night before, she had had a dream that something bad would happen in the water. Naturally, she assumed it would happen to the little kids.

The kids and I headed to the lake and settled in on the main beach next to the clubhouse. There were a number of people there, but it wasn't crowded. I sat on my towel under one of the trees at the edge of the sand as the kids swam and played. The sounds of water splashing and children laughing made for a pleasant afternoon. While I was watching the kids from up on shore, Jonathan called from the water, "David, come down and swim with me!"

"Okay," I yelled back. I took off my watch, shirt, and shoes, set them down on my towel, and ran down the sandy beach toward the water. The sun felt nice and warm on my chest. There were a few cute girls off to my left. *I hope I look good*, I thought. I ran into the water and dove in right next to my brother. Instantly, my head slammed into the sandy bottom, and just as instantly, my neck was broken and I was paralyzed.

That was it. That was all it took. In one innocent, happy moment, my life was changed forever.

I did not lose consciousness, as most people do after this kind of accident, but I stayed awake. I felt no pain. In those quiet and slow-motion couple of seconds face-down underwater, I thought, *I am paralyzed*. It's funny that I already knew. Not "funny" funny, just interesting. I had never known anyone in a wheelchair. I think that just from watching the news and television, plus having read Joni Eareckson's autobiography (the amazing story of a young woman who became a quadriplegic from a diving accident), I had learned that if you dive incorrectly and hit your head, you may become a quadriplegic and live the rest of your life in a wheelchair. That was my first thought in that very quiet, still moment.

My second thought, still in those initial seconds underwater, was truly a gift from God. *Well, God will heal me.* In such a short moment in time, those two thoughts encompassed such deep realization and insight that God's grace would guide me through whatever was to come.

While I was at peace in the quiet under the water, not being able to move my body and turn myself over, Jonathan saw my still body facedown. This was a crucial moment that determined whether I lived or died. He looked at my immobile body, and he thought I was pretending to be hurt. He had never before seen me injured. Of course, he would assume this moment was no different. I was the older brother he idolized, and in his mind, I was invincible. But, *THANK GOD*, he turned me over and sarcastically asked, "Oh, are you hurt?"

I took a breath of air. Out of the corner of my eye, I spotted my right arm floating listlessly beside me. I tried to move it—an instinctual, normal, everyday action—but nothing happened. I couldn't even feel it. I tried harder, willing the fingers to move. Nothing. A wave slapped me in the face, and with it came complete realization. *Wow, it's for real! I AM paralyzed.*

"Yes," I replied in a weak voice.

Jonathan still thought I was pretending to be hurt.

I looked him in the eye and said, "I'm dead serious." That comment and look hit home and struck my little brother to the core.

He quickly realized I was not playing around, and he placed his arms under my body to hold me up. He called the lifeguard, and together they carefully moved me toward the shore. In a random thought, I was impressed that the lifeguard, just a young guy my age, had the intelligence and training to keep my head and neck still, even though, of course, the damage to my spine had already been done.

As I lay there on the beach, I heard a woman call out, "Someone get a blanket!" Within seconds, I watched a blanket being placed over my body, but I felt nothing. I was thinking, *I don't need a blanket. I'm fine!* My body was, of course, already going into shock. Thank God for that natural response to physical trauma. You may have heard of stories where someone cutting lumber or wood suddenly sees a finger on the ground and doesn't even realize that it is his own. Well, basically, that is what I experienced, and once again, I thank God that I didn't feel any pain.

Laying there on the sand with a few people huddled around me, I soon heard the sirens getting louder, signaling the arrival of the paramedics. As they lifted me into the ambulance, I still remained calm. In fact, my thoughts were so elsewhere that I asked a bystander, "Will you please keep an eye on the kids I am babysitting? And my wristwatch and shoes are next to the tree." She must have thought that last request to be a bit odd, but being injured was all new to me.

While riding in the ambulance, I watched the paramedic hover over me. I tried to see myself from his perspective. I was a kid who had just suffered a very traumatic injury and I should be pretty sad about it. I had never experienced a serious injury before. I did not know how to respond in this situation. So, in order to somehow fulfill my impression of this paramedic's expectations, I tried to cry. In a whimpering voice, I asked, "Am I ever going to walk again?"

"I don't know," he replied.

Hmmm. Well, that was all the pretending I could muster, and my time of fake crying was over.

I was rushed to the local hospital, Grass Valley's only hospital, Sierra Nevada Memorial. Immediately, the emergency room doctor did a brief examination on me. "Can you wiggle your fingers? Can you move your toes? Can you move your legs?" I tried. Lying flat on my back with my head strapped to the gurney so that I could not move my neck, I tried, but I couldn't turn my head to see how successful I was. I could not feel my fingers or toes or legs. I knew, though, that whatever he asked me to move did not move and could not move.

Failing that simple test, I was transferred to Radiology for a series of x-rays. No one offered to share the results with me, but by my instincts and the looks on their faces, I already knew that the results weren't good.

A short time later, while I was waiting on a gurney in the ER by myself, my dad Richard rushed into the room.

"Hey, pal," he said compassionately.

"Hi, Dad," I replied.

We didn't get to say more, for at that moment, a nurse ushered him out to speak with my doctor. He returned a few minutes later, looking much more somber, and said, "We're going to get you the best care possible."

It was obvious that the doctors were now well aware of the severity of my injury. In fact, they had already called for the immediate takeoff of the Life Flight helicopter from the University of California at Davis (UCD) Medical Center, the nearest major trauma center. Upon learning about this transfer, my dad immediately got in his car and rushed to UCD to meet me there. Within the hour, I was loaded onto the helicopter and heading to Sacramento. The flight was so loud, bumpy, and hot that it was difficult for me to process, much less focus on, the gravity of my situation. I do remember keeping calm and quiet for the ride. Maybe I was at peace. Maybe I was blissfully doped up on medication.

As soon as I landed on the Life Flight pad, I was rushed through the doors of the Emergency Center. Even though I had already had a few hours to get some level of clarity, reality was about to hit me square in the face. Watching a team of very frantic doctors and nurses hovering over me, I was about to come to grips with how serious my injury really was.

First, I was plugged into numerous monitors that checked my heart rate, blood pressure, and oxygen level. Then the ER doctor wasted no time in examining my neck and my x-rays from Sierra Nevada Memorial Hospital. He explained, "When your head hit the sand, the impact squished the vertebrae in your neck like an accordion. Before any procedures or surgeries can be done, these vertebrae need to be decompressed. We need to stretch your neck, basically. I'm going to temporarily attach a brace to your head with a weight hanging from it that will slowly decompress your vertebrae. Over the next few days, another weight will be added every twelve hours, slowly stretching your vertebrae apart in preparation for surgery. Okay? Do you have any questions?"

"No, thank you," I answered.

"Okay, then. You're going to feel a pinch as I numb the side of your head."

Ooouuuccchhh!

Needles were inserted into the skin on either side of my head to numb the areas where holes would be bored into my skull in preparation for where a horseshoe-shaped brace would be bolted in. The pain from the needles was indescribable. I had never felt pain like that before. When the sides of my head were numb, the doctor began to "drill" into my skull to attach the brace. I did not feel it. My full memory of the incident though is cloudy. Perhaps it is due to the medication they had given me at the time. I do, however, remember the initial pain. My mom remembers that, for a long time, my eyes would water just recalling this first episode into my new life as a quadriplegic.

My mom's clearer memory of that time adds an informative and emotional perspective. As I have shared, the reason I had been babysitting that day was because my mom had driven to Sacramento to arrange her class schedule for college. Before she arrived back home with barbeque fixings and a cake to celebrate her big day, I had already been flown by helicopter from Grass Valley to the UCD Medical Center. So upon arriving home and finding her boys still gone, she assumed there must be a lot of cute girls at the lake that day and that I was having a great time.

As she recalls, the phone began ringing off the hook with friends calling. Each one asked if she was home alone, to which she replied, "Yes, but the boys will be home any minute." When each friend realized she was alone, no one wanted to be the one to tell her the real news about my accident. Finally, a very close friend called, and my mom, in desperation, insisted that she tell her why everyone was calling.

Helen reluctantly told her all she, or anyone else, knew. "There has been an accident at the lake."

"Adam? Jonathan?" my mom immediately asked, assuming it was one of them, since they were younger and more prone to accidents. Besides, I had played sports all my life, even in England, and had hardly gotten a scratch. I was the last one on her mind who would have injured himself.

Then her friend corrected her. "No, it's David."

"David?! What could have happened to David?"

Within a few minutes, several friends arrived to drive my mom back down to Sacramento. The trip down was quiet. No one quite realized the full seriousness of what had happened. In fact, all my mom could come up with was that I had probably just broken my arm.

Arriving at the Emergency Center, she wasted no time in finding someone who looked like medical personnel. When this nurse heard her say, "I am David Kline's mother," a doctor appeared almost out of thin air. My mom remembers him as looking too young to be a doctor. "I am sorry to give you this news," he said, "but your son might be paralyzed."

The lioness heart of a mother took over. "You do not use the word '*paralyzed*' in the same sentence as my son's name! You do not know him. You do not know the athlete he is. HE has played soccer in England. Don't you dare use

THAT word when you speak of him, my firstborn son!" Then she demanded to see me.

This young whippersnapper doctor told her, "Oh, no, you can't possibly see him now."

My mom responded, "I want to see my son."

Maybe he realized she was going to win this one, because with a look of resignation, he said, "Okay. Follow me," as he led her into the bowels of the Emergency Center. My mom will never forget the moment he pulled back the curtain. Her last memory of me before she had left that morning was handing me a picnic basket and wishing us a great day. Now, seeing me lying on a gurney with blood dripping from the two freshly drilled holes in my skull onto the linoleum floor, she was stunned.

I guess I gave her a measure of relief when I greeted her with, "Hi, Mom."

In that terrifying moment, hearing me call her by name, her immediate thought was that she didn't know what we were facing as far as my physical injuries were concerned, but at least she knew "We all still have 'David'. "Thankfully, I had no brain injury that would have compounded, at a much greater level, all that now lay ahead.

Relieved, she was escorted into another room as the emergency team took me to be evaluated by MRIs, brain scans, and numerous other tests for the next five hours. During all these tests, I remained quiet. I let them do what they needed to do.

When the tests were completed, a nurse wheeled me on my gurney to Neurointensive Care. There was a lot of activity in this section of the hospital, and it was brightly lit. My room was small and crowded with medical equipment. There was a window to the outside; the curtain was closed.

The opposite wall of my room was glass so that nurses could easily look in from the nurses' station. There was a full curtain along the glass wall that could be closed for privacy. A rocking chair sat empty in the corner for family members. My gurney was parked with the head against the solid wall, and I was reconnected to the various monitoring devices. My nurse took my vitals and then left. I waited alone.

My nurse soon returned. Because I was flat on my back and could not move, I was susceptible, like any spinal cord injury (SCI) patient, to pneumonia and to skin breakdown on my back, bottom, and heels. The doctor, knowing the proper procedure in injuries like mine, arranged for me to be placed onto a rotating air bed. "The mattress fills with air. The rotating function of the bed will slowly rotate side-to-side, like a cradle," my nurse informed me. That sounded pretty nice. "It will help prevent mucus from collecting in your lungs, and it will not allow too much pressure on any one area of your body."

The rotating bed was wheeled into my room and placed up against my gurney. I could not see it, but apparently it was quite a machine. It was a massive bed, tall and thick. Four nurses pulled my "draw sheet" and carefully slid me from the gurney onto the new bed. It felt like a regular bed. Though when it was plugged in and turned on, I could immediately feel the mattress filling up with air and lifting me up. This bed made quite a hum. At least it was a nicer sound than the annoying beeps from all the machines I was hooked up to.

"Ready for the rotating?" my nurse asked. I heard a faint, high-pitched whine and could feel my bed slowly tilt to the right. It reached its farthest point, not too far, and began its rotation to the left. *Not too bad.* I recalled Joni Eareckson's autobiography and her description of the bed she was on while in the hospital. *At least this bed is nothing like the bed she was on!* She described the Stryker frame, the bed used in the 1970s that served the same purpose as my rotating bed. Not only did a Stryker frame rock back and forth like mine, but it could even swing upside down, with the patient strapped to it, of course. Seriously. My thoughts? *That sounds awful! That sounds completely awful! I'm content with this bed.*

My doctor returned to attach the weight to my head brace. He hung a very small weight over the head of the bed, hanging on a wire from the brace toward the floor. Thankfully, the weight was so small that I did not notice much of a tug or strain at all, but I knew the increased weight over the coming days could become uncomfortable.

While I was upstairs, my mom and dad were being comforted and counseled by a team of grief specialists, doctors, and nurses. The staff gently educated them on the extent and implications of my injury. Later, my mom and dad were met by a team of researchers from Harvard Medical School to discuss the possibility of admitting me into a national research project on the effects of different drug therapies on fresh spinal cord injuries. Patients were randomly placed into one of three groups for this clinical trial. One group received the current steroid drug, one an experimental steroid, and the third group received a placebo. The study was entering the second year of a four-year study. We would not know which drug I would be administered for another four years.

The researchers required a parent's permission, because I was only seventeen at the time. What a decision for my mom and dad to be facing, having just been confronted with my catastrophic injury. So they did what any parent would do. "Forget the trial! Just give my son the new stuff!"

The researchers explained that that wasn't possible; they were not permitted to decide who would get the experimental steroid. With a prayer in their hearts, my parents agreed to allow me to be part of the study.

Then, for what seemed like an endless three hours, they sat in a waiting room. Finally, a nurse appeared and led them into the elevator. When the doors opened, they stepped into the Neurointensive Care Unit, which would be our home for the next three weeks.

Silently, they came into my small, dimly lit room and looked across at me. I was lying on my back on a rotatingbed. They saw the horseshoe brace attached to my head. They saw the short extension over the end of the bed. They saw the wire hanging from it to the floor, holding the first half-pound weight. My mom sat down in the rocking chair as she stared at the scene before her. In the darkness and above the bed's humming, she heard me ask one simple question, "Mom, are you there?"

"Yes, honey, I'm here," she replied, knowing she would stay in that room, and by my side, for as long as I needed her.

I couldn't turn my head to see the tears falling down her cheeks.

A short time later, a doctor entered the room, introduced himself, and told us that he was going to examine me. As I mentioned earlier, I knew the instant that my head hit the sand that I was paralyzed. I knew I no longer could move or even feel most of my body. Now, with a neurosurgeon, I would learn the extent of how much sensation I had, or didn't have, anymore. I watched him pull out a simple safety pin. He began to gently poke my feet. I couldn't be completely sure, because lying flat on my back, I couldn't see my feet. However, I could see where he was standing and assumed that he was starting on my feet. "Feel anything?" he asked.

"Nope," I replied.

I could tell that he was working his way up, because every few seconds, he would ask again, "Anything?"

"Nope." This continued for some time. Eventually, when he was standing right next to my chest, I said, "Maybe. I think I just barely felt something." He was poking my chest right above the nipple line. He continued up my chest, and with each poke, my sensation increased until I exclaimed, "Ouch!" My upper chest and everything above had normal sensation. He then progressed down my arms, poking as he went. My sensations were spotty, ending in no sensation in my hands. That was it for sensation—as in, not much.

He then asked me to try to wiggle my toes. I tried. I didn't see a pleasantly surprised smile on his face, so I knew that my toes had not moved. He asked me to try to move my fingers. I tried. Nothing. I could barely shrug my shoulders and barely use my biceps. That was it. I couldn't use my fingers. I couldn't use my legs. I had no control of any muscles below my chest.

When he was finished, he gave his overall diagnosis. "Your level of sensation is fairly typical with a C-5 injury. Some patients have minimal loss, which can be good and bad. These patients might experience a great deal of pain. Most patients with injuries as high up the spine as yours lose a majority of their body's sensation. There is a chance though that, over the next twelve months, as the swelling around your injury decreases, you might regain some sensation. Your movement is also very limited. You may see a slight increase in movement and strength over time."

Wow. I guess it wasn't anything I haven't already realized. He did, however, mention the possibility of increased sensation and movement. That sounded good. I hope that happens to me.

I really took this calmly, considering the seriousness of my injury. I hadn't freaked out. I hadn't panicked. I'm not exactly sure why. I know that some of it was due to my faith in God. I also think that some of my acceptance was due to the fact that I just didn't really know anything about spinal cord injuries except that there was nothing I could do at that moment to change anything or to make it better. At that moment in time on that day, *that* was my condition—*that* was my physical status. It might improve tomorrow or the next day or the next day. We'll see.

There were many people who were also hoping that I would see physical improvement. Little did I know that, at that very moment, family friends had driven more than an hour to the hospital just to sit in the waiting room to support me and to pray for me. Coach Kopec and his wife Vicki were there. Our family friend and chiropractor, Dale Jacobson, and his wife Diane were there, as well as many others.

In those first hours at UCD Med Center, I was never told, "You will never walk again," like the way you see doctors on TV bluntly announce to their patients. Like I shared, from the moment my head hit the sand, I already knew the potential extent of my injury when it happened. Now, in ICU, with all the x-rays and the horseshoe brace screwed into my skull, gently and slowly pulling my vertebrae apart, it was clear that my neck was seriously damaged. Within a few days, I would be wheeled into surgery for the operation that would stabilize my spinal cord.

Unless one has known someone with a spinal injury, most of us do not quite understand how an injury to the spinal cord can have such devastating effects on the body. To give a sense of how and why that happens, here's my simple explanation. The spinal cord is a pathway of nerves that connects the brain to every part of the body. It runs from the base of the brain all the way down the middle of the back. I like to compare it to the thick wires on telephone poles. When that thick wire is cut in half, one can see that there are hundreds of tiny wires inside that one thick wire. I'll admit that this analogy is not entirely accurate since the inside of the spinal cord actually contains numerous columns, tracts, and bundles of various sizes.

Nerves branch off from the spinal cord to every part of the body. If someone wants to move his right foot, that message will travel down the spinal cord and out to the foot muscles to move that foot. And if someone is sitting too close to a stove and his foot is getting too warm, the message of "too hot" will travel up his leg, up his spinal cord, and into his brain, telling him he had better move his foot before it burns. If the spinal cord is damaged or cut, then messages from or to the brain will be limited or even impossible.

Protecting this valuable and vulnerable spinal cord is the spinal column. These bones, called vertebrae, surround the entire length of the spinal cord. When I dove into the water and smashed my head into the sand, I crushed the spinal column so severely that I mangled my spinal cord at the fifth cervical. The medical diagnosis is quadriplegia, meaning four limbs have lost all or partial movement.

The result of my injury is fairly typical with what would be expected, meaning I have use of a certain, limited number of muscles and a lack of feeling in the parts of my body consistent with my level of injury. I have no feeling from the chest down. For most people, it is difficult to comprehend or imagine losing almost all of one's physical sensation. The best way that I can explain how it feels when I try to move my legs is to describe a situation that most people have experienced. I think most people have been to the beach, dug a large hole in the sand, and buried themselves in it up to their waists. Then they tried to break free and pull their legs out. At first, their legs were stuck, but they could tell that they were trying and trying, but nothing was happening. That's how it feels.

Generally, the higher up that the spinal cord is injured, the less muscle function and the less bodily physical sensation the injured person has. For example, Christopher Reeve, Superman, broke his neck at the first and second cervical, thus he could not move his arms. He also required a ventilator to help his lungs function so that he could breathe. An injury so close to the brain stem often results in the immediate death of the injured person. In fact, when a person is hanged, his neck often breaks at the first or second cervical, thus killing him. There is not much distance between my injury (the fifth cervical) and the first or second cervical. I was fortunate to be alive and fortunate to breathe without a ventilator.

The reason spinal cord injuries are so permanent is because spinal cord cells do not regenerate. For example, if you get a cut on your arm, it will scab over and eventually heal. Unfortunately, spinal cord cells do not heal; they just stay broken. Scientists are trying various new technologies to get spinal cord cells to regrow. Some people have wondered, "If your spinal cord cannot be repaired, why did the doctors want to perform surgery?" Well, this surgery was not to fix the nerves or the spinal cord but to fix and stabilize the broken spinal column.

All that information about the spinal cord I learned later. I was pretty out of it at this point. I was able though to understand that I needed surgery to stabilize my neck. I was immediately placed on the schedule for surgery.

It was the middle of the night at this point, and things started to "settle down" for me. "Settle down" still included nurses coming in frequently to check on me and my vitals. My mom curled up on the rocking chair with a blanket one of the nurses brought in for her. The lights were dimmed in the hallway and in my room, and I listened to the numerous noises and beeps and hums of the medical equipment that kept my lungs filling with air and monitored my condition.

I did not sleep much that night. That was the first day of my life as a quadriplegic.

CHAPTER 4

At six o'clock the next morning, I was already awake and could hear the day-shift nurses arriving and checking in with the night-shift nurses at the nurses' station just outside my room. All the hallway lights were turned on. Within a few minutes, a nurse came in and introduced herself.

"How are you doing?" she asked pleasantly.

"Fine," I replied.

She checked my vitals, and then she left. She seemed nice.

Before long, she returned and told me that she was going to help me urinate. I didn't have the sensation that I needed to pee, but then again, I didn't have much sensation at all. I actually hadn't even thought about peeing with everything else my mind was occupied with. She told me that a catheter had been inserted into my bladder during last night's marathon of procedures. This catheter, she explained, had been connected to a drainage bag. From the side of the bed, she held up the bag, which was now nearly full. "Your doctor would like your bladder to be on a schedule of draining every six hours from now on," she told me. She lifted up the bed sheet and began the process of catheterization.

I was somewhat embarrassed by the fact that a woman I didn't even know had lifted up my sheet and was doing whatever catheterization was "down there." I was always pretty modest about that kind of stuff. Given I had no choice, I just figured that this was something that had to be done for my survival and well-being. She was just doing her job. Unfortunately, she didn't explain to me what she was doing or what the process involved; she just started. I was flat on my back and couldn't see what she was doing, but I could hear her opening papers and packages.

Can I at least have a brief word of explanation, please? I thought to myself.

After a couple of minutes, she finished draining my bladder and began to clean up the materials that she used. I caught just a glimpse of her hand holding red soaked tissue and gauze. *Yikes!* It startled me and kind of freaked me out, but I didn't say anything. I didn't have any prior experience or knowledge about hospitals or injuries or catheters, so I just assumed that catheterization caused bleeding and that, again, was just the way it goes.

So many things were being done to my body, and I had no control or say over any of them. I knew they *had* to be done, but still, I felt powerless about what was being done to my own body. I didn't feel frustrated or angered by this though. I was just trying to come to grips with my new reality.

My mom came back into my room. She had stepped out briefly when the day-shift nurses had arrived earlier.

My mom had stayed by my side all night in the rocking chair, not sleeping. We were relieved to see each other.

My neurosurgeon entered. Greeting both of us, he asked how I was doing.

I replied, "Fine."

He proceeded to inform us that my surgery had been placed on the schedule for Saturday, three days away.

He examined both sides of my head where the brace was attached. "Looks good. I'm going to add a little more weight now."

I felt a slight tug on my head and neck, but nothing too bad.

"I'll check in on you again soon," he said as he left.

Unbeknown to me, that morning the hospital had tracked down the phone number of my biological father, Jack. He rushed right over and was led into my room. It was good for me to see him. From his perspective, he saw an injured, weak, frightened boy. He sat with my mom and me for hours.

Because I had been x-rayed last night and my injury diagnosed, my second day as a quadriplegic was less hectic than the first. The focus now was on my surgery on Saturday and maintaining my current level of stability until then. So throughout the day, the only activity was various doctors and nurses checking in on me and my vitals. My mom stayed by my side for the rest of the day.

Later that day, my night nurse entered my room and asked my mom if she could excuse us for a few moments while she helped me catheterize (drain my bladder). Unlike my day nurse, this nurse explained everything she was doing. One of the steps she described aloud, "Now I'm cleaning with iodine." Out of the corner of my eye, I saw her set down a "bloody" cotton ball.

Ohhh, it's iodine! Phew! No blood involved "down there!"

Like the previous morning, I was already awake at 6 a.m. when the hospital came alive. My mom and my dad Richard immediately came in to check on me. Following them was my day nurse who greeted all of us and then did what every nurse seemed to do first when entering my room—check my vitals. She then removed my covers so she could examine my body. Right at that moment, a group of people entered my room. I recognized one of my doctors among them. I made eye contact with my dad and whispered, "Am I naked?" He nodded. I responded with an embarrassed smile. My doctor introduced me to the medical students who were making their morning rounds. *Well, since they're medical students, I guess it's kind of okay that I'm naked.* He then began to tell them all about my accident, my current condition, and my upcoming surgery. It was all information I was aware of. The students were taking notes and discussing my condition with my doctor. This "student lesson" became a routine every morning at 6 a.m. My parents were even allowed to be there to listen.

That afternoon, my mom informed me that Jonathan hadn't stopped crying since he got home the night of my accident and that he really wanted to see me. It crushed me to hear that he was so distraught, and I, too, longed to see my brothers. My parents had been hesitant to let them see me due to my "gruesome" condition—my shaved head, the metal contraption drilled into my skull, numerous wires and monitors, and my weakened body. Finally, my parents gave in and told Jonathan he could see me that day; Adam would have to wait until I was more stable.

My dad brought Jonathan up the elevator to my floor. As they were walking down the hallway toward my room, I was being wheeled out of my room on a gurney to get a scheduled x-ray in preparation for my surgery the next day. My nurse paused as we passed each other, just long enough for Jonathan to get a look at his "invincible" older brother. It was a sight Jonathan has never forgotten. I wasn't able to turn my head to look at him, but I stated, "Jon, thank you for helping me at the beach." That was all that was said, and my nurse continued pushing me to Radiology.

It was a heartbreaking scene. I wished I could've talked with him, comforted him, and let him know I was okay.

Four days after my accident, it was finally time for surgery on my spine. I was ready and mentally prepared. I knew the seriousness, the reality, and the necessity of the surgery. I'm not sure my mom was so calm. My dad Richard and my father Jack were by her side for this event, so as I was wheeled into the elevator, all three were standing by me. And all three were there when I passed through the double doors into the surgical suite. My mom recalls that each door had a small window, enough to watch me as I disappeared around the corner into the unknown.

From what I could see from lying on my back, the operating room was fairly large. An enormous bedlike contraption was resting on the ceiling in the center of the room. Monitors, medical equipment, and trays were scattered throughout. The temperature in the room was a bit cool for me. My gurney was parked adjacent to the operating table. A number of nurses and three or four doctors introduced themselves to me. Four of the nurses carefully slid me onto the operating table. I was now directly under the bed attached to the ceiling. All my monitors and wires were then connected to the operating room equipment. My neurosurgeon entered and greeted me. He sounded positive and upbeat.

Here we go!

First, I had to be anesthetized. This was the first time in my life that I needed anesthesia, so I had no prior experience to compare it to. I wasn't worried. The anesthesiologist stood next to me and said, "Okay, I will be administering the medication now." I waited expectantly for a sensation of drifting off to sleep. A few minutes later, he began shoving tubes down my throat, but I was not knocked out yet! *Wait, I'm still awake! Wait!* Before I really could react, I was out. That was a horrible experience.

Once I was unconscious, the bed from the ceiling was mechanically lowered down over me until I was sandwiched between it and the surgical bed. This sandwich was then flipped (rotated 180 degrees) over. The top bed lifted up to the ceiling, leaving me facedown on the other bed. The back of my neck was now accessible for surgery.

Next, the neurosurgeon made his incision in my neck, and he saw inside that I had totally mangled and severed my nerves and had crushed my fifth vertebrae to bits. Previous MRIs had already made him aware of this, so in order to fix the problem of my destroyed vertebrae, he removed a chip of bone off my hip and inserted it into my neck at the location of the break. Then he fused and wired that bone to the healthy cervical bones above and below it.

Now that my neck was stabilized, my surgeon needed to make sure that it healed and remained stable. When a person breaks his arm, doctors will place the arm in a cast so that the bones will heal properly. Since there is no way to cast the neck, doctors attach a "halo" brace. Envision a medieval torture device, and you'll have a good idea.

The brace does resemble a halo, because a metal ring encircles the patient's head. Protruding from the halo are four screws. To attach the halo to my head, my neurosurgeon drilled four holes into my skull, with two screws in the back and two in the front, just above each eyebrow. To ensure that my neck would remain still, my neurosurgeon then attached the halo to four metal rods, two in the front of my body and two in the back. These rods were attached to a brace placed around my chest. The halo, rods, and brace would keep my neck perfectly straight while it healed after the surgery. The hospital sounds like a fun place, doesn't it?

This surgery was very complicated and delicate, requiring six hours to complete. Metaphorically speaking, I had just taken the first step in my long and arduous recovery.

The day after my surgery, my head was hurting. "Mom, my head doesn't feel good," I said to her. "The halo brace feels really heavy."

"I'm sorry, honey," she replied. "The halo must weigh a lot. This is just the first day. Let's see if it will get better."

I agreed. I was quiet for some time. My mom continued to sit by my side.

"Mom?"

"Yes, honey?"

"Will my friends still want to be my friends?"

"Why, yes, of course!" my mom answered, grieving in her heart that I was worrying about losing my friends while at the same time worrying about what the rest of my life would look like.

It was very comforting for me to have my mom there. Because she was sticking by my side for as much time as was allowed, one of the nice nurses brought in a more comfortable chair for her that evening. My mom was learning that there were nice nurses and mean nurses. The mean nurses would not allow any visitors and would not allow my mom to stay with me after visiting hours. The nice nurses let my mom stay beyond visiting hours. They even let her sleep on the couch in their break room at night. If I would ask for my mom in the middle of the night, the nice nurses would go get her for me. From the first night, my mom lived at the hospital. Every evening when my nurse was in my room taking care of me, my mom's friends met her outside on the lawn with homemade dinners. Their support and breathing in the fresh air kept her going through it all.

The next afternoon, my brother Adam convinced our parents to allow him to see me. My dad escorted them in. Jon was more mentally prepared this time, as he had already experienced the initial shock of my injured appearance. Adam was brave though and approached my bedside. I strained my eyes over to see him, and I gave him a smile, saying in a low, weak voice, "Hi, Adam."

He smiled back as best he could. The three of us boys and Dad spent the afternoon together there in my hospital room. The time and the smiles relaxed the mood and the anxiety my brothers felt earlier. It was wonderful for me to see them, spend time with them, and comfort them.

Two days after my surgery, my doctors explained it was necessary to place a number of tubes down my throat.

They told me that one tube, a feeding tube, will go down into my stomach, a second tube will go into my lungs to pump in oxygen so that I can breathe better, and a third will go into my lungs to suck out any mucus that had built up. Inserting the tubes turned out, once again, to be a very uncomfortable procedure. One at a time, each tube made me choke as it passed my gag reflex. The pain and the gagging made tears stream from my eyes. *Why didn't they do this two days ago when I was unconscious?!* I didn't fight it though, for I understood the absolute necessity of each tube. The insertion of the tubes only took a few minutes, but what a painful, frightening, and exhausting experience!

Unfortunately, all the tubes going down my throat presented a new problem—I was not able to speak. This, obviously, was very frustrating. Because I couldn't move my hands, couldn't talk, and couldn't nod or shake my head, blinking became my only means of communication. But even this was too complicated for some of my nurses.

One day my nurse and I agreed that one blink would mean "yes" and two blinks would mean "no". Unfortunately, she didn't tell my night nurse this very brief but very important information. That night, my nurse began to poke and prod and asked, "Does this hurt?" It certainly did hurt, so I quickly made very exaggerated, single and slow blinks. "Good," she said, thinking I was blinking "no," and continued with her "torture." *It hurts!* I screamed in my head. *One blink means "Yes, it hurts!"*

The next day, my day nurse remembered our rules. *Good.* As the night shift arrived, I thought, *Please, ladies, share this simple arrangement with each other. Please.* The poking and prodding began. Again she asked, "Does this hurt?" I blinked once. *Get this right.* "Good," she said and continued poking. *Aaarrrggghhh! How hard is it to figure this out! Make a sign explaining the blinks and put it above my bed for everyone to see. You guys are the educated ones! I'm just a kid! I'm just the patient! Come on!*

Not being able to talk and not being able to be understood was incredibly frustrating. I gained a sense of sympathy for people who faced this frustration regularly.

The next day, a therapist suggested that we use the alphabet for my communication. *Thank you!* Now, to communicate, a doctor, nurse, parent, etc. would slowly say the letters of the alphabet to me. I would blink at each letter that was in the word I wanted to communicate. The therapist began the process so that I could communicate my first word. She said, "A." I didn't blink. She said, "B." I didn't blink. This pattern continued like this for quite some time. Finally, at the letter *M*, I blinked twice. She wrote *M M* on a small erase board. I blinked once at the letter *O*. My therapist went and got my mom for me.

With my mom now present, I attempted to blink my second word. I blinked *E, O, O, R*. My mom grinned as she guessed the word and said, "OREO". I guess a week on tube feeding really stirred up my sweet tooth. If I could have smiled with all those tubes in my mouth, this brief, simple moment would have brought on my first smile since my accident seven days ago. I was smiling on the inside though.

CHAPTER 5

I was due for some real joy. This had been a pretty miserable and gloomy time. My next "inside smile" appeared shortly thereafter when my dad showed up with my "sister," Shelley. Only family members were allowed to visit in ICU, and Shelley certainly counted! The muscles around the tubes in my mouth clinched tightly as a smile automatically tried to form. I was so thrilled to see her and her great smile! Her smile successfully hid the fright she felt inside at her first sight of me in my injured state with the halo and tubes and medical equipment.

Obviously, we hadn't gotten to go on our date. I wanted to make a joke about this being our first date, but, of course, I couldn't talk with all the tubes in my mouth.

She told me about the day of my accident and how my dad had called her to tell her about my accident. It turned out, Shelley was the one who drove my car back to my house from the lake. I hadn't even thought about my car since I had been in the hospital.

After a while, Shelley was quiet, but she continued to sit by my side. With care, she held my hand from time to time, though I couldn't feel her touch. It was comforting to have her there. It was comforting to know that she wanted to be there.

Eventually, it was time for her to leave, as it was time for my nurse to help me with my catheter. "I'll visit again soon," Shelley said. "Love you."

Love you too, my eyes said.

Over a few days of all those tubes continually down my throat, my doctors began to become concerned that the tubes would damage my vocal cords. *It's just one thing after another.* The doctors decided that I should have a surgery called a tracheotomy. "I will make a small incision in the front of your neck in your airway so that the tubes can be inserted there instead of through your mouth," one doctor informed me as simply as he could. I understood what he was explaining, but I also naively assumed it was a much larger and permanent surgery. The doctor envisioned that these tubes would remain inserted for a couple of months and then be removed, allowing the opening in my neck to heal and close. He never told me this though.

I guess I'll have a hole in my throat for the rest of my life and have to talk through my throat with one of those microphone things, sounding all grainy and robotic. Well, if this is what has to be done, then I'll agree to the surgery.

"Yes," I blinked. I don't know why I assumed the microphone thing, for I was way off. I soon learned that people who have had a tracheotomy can talk through their mouth and don't need a throat microphone. *Phew!*

So, another surgery was scheduled. I was not looking forward to the anesthesia, remembering my terror at the onset of my previous surgery. Thankfully, this next experience with anesthesia was nowhere near as traumatic. When I regained consciousness, my mouth was clear of tubes, thankfully, and a "trach" (sort of a plastic valve) was left in my neck.

However, this didn't mean that I could now talk easily. The only way that airflow could travel past my vocal cords and out my mouth to produce words was if someone placed his/her finger over the "airhole" tube in the trach to block air from exiting there. So, I learned that when someone would ask me a question, then he/she would need to put her finger over my trach so that I could respond. Yes, it was kind of a hassle, but at least I could talk again.

Something that grossed me out though was when my friend Matt came to visit me a week later and I noticed his finger was really dirty when he first reached to block my trach; I didn't want someone's germs there! *Oh well.* I was learning that I was at other people's mercy, but because I was so nonconfrontational, I didn't complain, even as I imagined the wild party all those germs were having in my throat! I just welcomed the ability to speak and communicate more easily.

As if I didn't have enough duties to go through to stay healthy and to stay alive, another activity was added to my daily routine called "range of motion". To prevent my joints and muscles from getting tight and locking up, Ron Silver, the primary physical therapist at UCD, put me through a series of joint rotations and muscle stretches to keep everything flexible. Ron was an especially cheerful and helpful guy and made this "duty" a pleasant experience.

As he gently lifted each of my legs, then bent the knee a number of times, and then did the same to my arms, elbows, wrists, fingers, feet, and toes, he reminded me, "You have to do range of motion every day. I can't stress this enough. I once heard about a guy in a wheelchair who never ever stretched, and his muscles were so tight that when he was on his back in bed, his legs would remain stuck up in the air and bent as if he were still sitting."

Yikes! Stretches are definitely something I plan on doing every morning!

When I wasn't busy with doctors, nurses, or therapists, I listened to the TV in my room. I say "listened," because I was flat on my back with the rigid halo attached to my head and could only look up at the ceiling. Listening to the TV was, at least, some form of entertainment. More than that, it was probably a good distraction for me.

Eventually, one of my nurses brought me some special glasses so I could see the TV on the far wall. These glasses had small angled mirrors in place of lenses. Lying flat on my back and looking straight up, I could now see the TV in the mirrors of the glasses. *This is cool!* Unfortunately though, it didn't take long for the glasses to give me a headache. I kindly told my nurse, "Thank you, but no thank you."

I found additional entertainment and comfort in music. When I needed something relaxing and peaceful, I listened to Zamphir, the world-famous pan flute musician. My mom had picked up a cassette at the store and had brought my boom box from home. We played that tape over and over and over again. It was really soothing! There were other times when I listened to the song "Rocketman" by Elton John. I'll admit it's a great song, but I don't know where my obsession for it came from while in the hospital.

During my time in ICU, I didn't sleep. I don't mean I didn't sleep much; I mean I didn't sleep at all. I don't know if it was because of my new injury, but I do know that with all the medicine, the constant attention from doctors and nurses, the beeping machines, and the constant light in ICU, I just could not sleep. And to make it worse, it got to the point that every time I would close my eyes, I would instantly be hallucinating a nightmare. This was both scary and annoying. Apparently, not being able to sleep after an extended period of time in ICU is so common that it has been given a name: ICUitis. Seriously.

With the insomnia, the surgeries, the pain, the new disability, and everything else, my mom arranged a boost to my spirits. She told me she needed to leave for a minute but that she'd be right back. Her grin looked suspicious. Sure enough, about a minute later, she poked her head around the curtain. "I have a surprise for you." I couldn't talk without her finger on my trach, but my mind was certainly wondering what she was referring to. She pulled back the curtain, and there was my best friend, Scott. I could not contain the huge smile on my face!

"Hey, 'cousin'! Your mom told the nurses that we're related," he said, grinning. I kept smiling, my first smile without tubes in my mouth in ten days! Seeing him and listening to him as he caught me up on life back home was fantastic!

But his visit did something else for me. His visit anchored my life, my life before my accident. It reaffirmed that I still had a life and friends. Seeing Scott reassured me that I hadn't been forgotten. I was lying there thinking how good this felt when he pulled out a tape recorder and the tape from my answering machine filled with the messages from all my friends who had called my phone. He told me that my dad had been recording a new outgoing message every day with an update about my physical condition. Many friends called frequently to listen and to leave well wishes. I recognized each friend's voice instantly! I even heard a message from the Taco Queen from Sacramento.

Being that I was from such a small town and that so many people knew me, the messages went on and on and on. Some of my friends were saying funny things; some were consoling. There were just no words that captured how high I felt hearing their voices of love, friendship, and concern. Playing my newest phone messages became a regular ritual that kept me smiling and dreaming of when I could go home.

Scott then told us about some of the rumors circulating around town about my accident. "Some people think you jumped off a bridge or that you did a double backflip off a dock and hit your head on a rock."

I winked to signal that I had something to say. My mom put her finger over the airhole of my trach. In short broken breaths, I said, "At least those stories are more exciting than what really happened!" Breath. "Maybe I *do* need a more exciting story." Breath. "Maybe, from now on, I'll tell people I was a test pilot for the Air Force"—breath—"and that I was piloting a new top-secret jet"—breath—"which malfunctioned and crashed in the Nevada desert."

They both agreed that was a more exciting story.

Then my mom chimed in, "I was just so surprised that anything bad happened to you because you have always been so cautious."

Her comment led me back to thoughts I had been processing in my head lately. *In truth, my injury was not the result of me being stupid or careless. It was a regular kind of dive that everyone does into the water. I had overheard somewhere though that my brother might have been sitting on his knees, so maybe it looked to me like he was standing and that the water was deeper than it actually was. It doesn't matter. And I don't want my brother to ever feel responsible. Really, it was just a freak accident. I'm not placing the blame on anyone. I'm sure this accident happened for a reason. I have no doubt that good can happen from any circumstance.*

Well, this splendid afternoon visit came to an end when my nurse appeared to remind me I needed to rest. It was bittersweet saying good-bye to my silly, wonderful friend who had given me my best afternoon in quite a while.

After two exhausting weeks in ICU, I was told that I was stable enough to transfer to the regular floor of the hospital. *What a relief! Progress!* Oops. Wait a minute. Not so fast. One hour prior to my scheduled transfer time, a major complication arose. Due to my spinal cord injury, not only had my limbs been affected, but my lungs were paralyzed too. A few days before, I had already been placed on a ventilator, or breathing machine, because my lungs had weakened. And now, after two weeks of weakened lungs breathing in hospital germs, I learned that I had pneumonia. In fact, I had double pneumonia (I assumed correctly that this meant pneumonia in both lungs). This is very serious for anyone, but it is even more serious for a quadriplegic. My poor health, once again, meant my stay in ICU wasn't over yet. What a setback! *This is such a bummer! I want to get better!*

Within the hour, I listened as my new pulmonary doctor explained, "David, we need to quickly get you started on breathing treatments to loosen the mucus in your lungs. This will be a regular routine for you for a while." *Another routine. Okay, I can deal with it. That doesn't sound too bad.*

My naïveté and trust about "new treatments and routines" was about to take an unpleasant turn. A nurse came in with some new equipment, including a plastic mask, which she placed over my mouth and nose. The mask was connected to a small canister. "The fumes are medicated," she said, "and will help break up the thick mucus. Breathe in deeply."

It smells like sulfur. Well, if it's supposed to help, I'll do it, but it still smells like sulfur.

"I'll be back in about twenty minutes to take off your mask. Then we'll go on to the next step."

Hmmm, I wonder what the "next step" will be.

Those twenty minutes dragged on. She finally returned with two other people, one of whom was a physical therapist. They turned off the machine, which thankfully stopped the fumes, and then removed the mask. *Ahhh, fresh air!*

"We're now going to try to get any mucus out of your lungs that we can," the nurse said as they carefully turned me over onto my stomach and slid me up on the bed so that my head hung over the edge of the bed. Then they loosened the bars connecting my halo to my chest brace to allow greater flexibility (or some other insufficient reason).

Uh, is that wise to do? I wondered. My head hung so far over the head of the bed that I could read (upside down) the bed manufacturer's label written on the head of the bed. *This can't be good for a neck that is supposed to be healing and recovering from a spinal cord injury and spinal fusion! My spinal surgeons would freak out if they saw my pulmonary doctors and nurses doing this to me!* While I was in this position, the respiratory therapist suddenly began to pound on my back with his palms to try to loosen up the mucus. *Ugh! Ugh! Ugh!* I could feel the blows that were higher up on my back where I had sensation, but the lower ones were only felt through sound and the vibration they caused. The pounding seemed to go on forever.

Then it got scary. The combination of the medicinal fumes and the pounding actually worked as the doctor and nurses intended. Thick mucus worked its way up out of my lungs. Unfortunately, it then blocked my airway. *I can't breathe! I can't get any air! Do something!* The therapist continued pounding. *Help!* Finally, they turned me back over and shoved a suction tube down my throat, which started to suck out the mucus. *Almost there! Just hold on!* I told myself. Then my airway was clear, but my lungs were just too weak to take in deep breaths. *I still can't breathe!* A nurse quickly attached an Ambu Bag to my trach and forced air into my lungs. Finally, I could breathe! *Thank God!* I was exhausted, mentally and physically exhausted.

That treatment was so horrible that I really felt like I could die. My doctors, sensing my panic during the experience and listening to my comments afterward, told me that they would allow my mom to stay with me during the next treatments. That was comforting. They also told me, unfortunately, that I will have to go through this excruciating treatment every twelve hours.

Before my next treatment, I was so scared that I asked my nurses to pray for me. I, too, prayed and prayed and panicked and prayed again. My lungs were in such extremely weak condition that I knew I needed every little breath to survive, and I knew I did not even have the strength to cough any of the mucus up out of my airway. Those moments of no air were awful.

For the second treatment, in order to avoid any more of those awful moments, my mom lay on the floor under my head so that she could tell the doctors when it looked like I couldn't breathe. Sure enough, during that treatment and future treatments, she could see the panic on my face and had to tell the doctors that I needed the Ambu Bag for air immediately. She still recalls how horrible and heartbreaking each treatment was.

Every time I had to go through it, I would think to myself, *I've got to tell these doctors and nurses how to do this process better.* Hopefully they have found a better way to do this. On a lighter note, there is one thing I did speak up about and request of my doctors. I asked them if they could schedule these horrendous treatments either before or after *David Letterman* and reruns of *The Monkees* aired. I had to make sure I got some humor and laughs there in Intensive Care! Believe it or not, the doctors agreed.

Through those darkest moments of my lung treatments, my mom was such a help to me. Even during the quiet times there in the hospital, her presence was a comfort. When it was just the two of us, she helped me with a lot of the mental processing I had to do regarding my accident. I had many questions that needed answering.

One afternoon, I finally mustered up the courage to ask her an important question that I had been concerned about.

"Mom?" I asked after she placed her finger over the airhole of my trach.

"Yes, sweetie," she said.

"Can I still have children?"

"I don't know," she said. "But, you know what? We're in a teaching hospital. I'll go find out." With that, she left my room and headed out in search of the answer.

She came back about half an hour later. "I went to the Department of Urology and asked the doctor your question. Yes, you can have children."

That was a relief! That answer was another confirmation that it was possible for me to have a "regular" life as a quadriplegic.

On one of those days while it was just me and my mom and dad, suddenly everything just started to fade. I was blacking out. It felt good, peaceful, and restful. I blacked out. The alarms on the life support machines suddenly screeched loudly, and the lines of my heartbeat went flat on the screen.

My mom recalls trying to somehow telepathically tell me, "David, if you need to fly, fly, darling. Don't worry about me or anyone else. Just do what you need to do." I came back into consciousness and saw that my room was full of doctors and nurses. My eyes were wide open and intense, and she knew I wasn't ready to go and that I wanted to fight on.

Then it happened again. As I blacked out, my mom saw that my eyes were still open and full of panic as if I were saying to her, "Mom, don't you dare let them let me die!" I was awake again just as suddenly, and my vitals and condition were stabilized. Everyone in that room breathed a sigh of relief.

Obviously, a spinal cord injury and double pneumonia were very serious, life-threatening ailments, but I guess God wasn't through with me yet.

CHAPTER 6

Surprisingly, and thankfully, my health soon improved enough after a week that I was moved out of ICU. This was such a good move for so many different reasons. As I have shared, I didn't sleep at all during the three weeks in ICU. I was exhausted, and my mind was cloudy. *I hope that now I will be able to sleep.*

I was placed on a regular hospital bed, so I no longer had to endure the humming and rotating of the previous bed. It was also quieter in this wing of the hospital. There was less rushing about. I was fortunate again to be placed in my own room. All my get-well cards and flowers came with me, which reminded me how much I was loved. I had also received quite a collection of T-shirts as gifts. My latest was a Life Flight T-shirt from the helicopter pilots who flew me here.

Now that I was out of ICU, my doctor wanted to check a measurement that hadn't been checked yet—my weight. Before my accident, when I was a junior in high school, all of the students in my Physical Education class were tested for body fat percentage. I weighed about 140 pounds and measured at 3.5 percent body fat, which is a very low body fat percentage. I won't say I was skinny; I prefer the term *slim*. I was pretty much muscle, skin, and bones. *I'm sure I've lost weight by now,* I thought. I had heard of atrophy. I knew that not being able to move and lying flat on my back in a hospital bed for three weeks would certainly cause muscle loss. Two nurses wheeled a gurney next to my bed. The gurney was fitted with a flat scale for weighing patients while lying down. Then they both lifted and transferred me onto the scale. "One hundred ten pounds," a nurse said.

Wow! Wow. Hmm. I was sad. I was quiet. *Sigh.* I dealt with it. *It's just another thing in a long list of crummy news. But there's nothing I can do about it.* Thirty pounds of my muscles had just wasted away. It really doesn't take long to lose muscle. My mom told me later that she could see my muscles disappearing by the third day after my accident. It's true what they say, "Use it or lose it."

Despite that sad news, I was happy to see other aspects of my physical condition improving and stabilizing. My breathing and lung capacity were now strong enough that I no longer needed to be on a ventilator. This was great! I could finally talk on my own without somebody having to block my trach.

Then, one day, quite unexpectedly, my neurosurgeon wanted to take off my halo. *I thought I remember him telling me that halos are typically left on for months. He wants to take it off after only three weeks?! Is my neck even ready?! Is it strong enough? Will my head fall off?* I am all for progressive therapy and for health care based on new and advanced research, but this news from my surgeon really startled and scared me. My parents were just as concerned as I was. My surgeon merely explained to us that I was ready and did not need to wait any longer.

Well, let's hope the doctor knows what he's doing! I agreed to his plan. I wasn't anticipating a very pleasant experience. I remember quite well the pain involved when the screws of the first brace were going in; I'm sure there's some discomfort when taking them out. My mom was there for me, as usual. My best friend's brother, Mark, was also there that afternoon for a visit. I allowed him to stay, for I didn't think this would be too big of a deal. I was wrong.

As the doctor began pulling the screws out of my head, I painfully yelled, "Are you screwing them in further?" Out of the corner of my eye, I saw Mark faint onto the floor. *Oh, yeah. I forgot that he faints at the slightest sight of blood or anything medical.* I think that that brief, comedic moment helped take my mind off the pain. Well, when it was all said and done, Mark was fine, and my head didn't fall off.

My family, my friends, my doctors and nurses, and I were quite relieved that I had survived these critical stages. The hospital had not been a fun place for me. Surprise, surprise. I had never experienced such pain in my life. But I was slowly getting through the necessary steps of recovery, and that's a good thing. I was hopeful that far greater progress lay ahead of me.

My next hurdle was to sit up. Seriously. I know that sounds so simple, but I had been flat on my back for more than three weeks. I had spent so much time on my back that I would count ceiling tiles, as I'm sure most long-term patients do to keep from going crazy. I would even look for similar patterns in the predrilled holes in the ceiling tiles. That sounds crazy!

After spending so much time flat on my back, I also started to get the typical bald spot on the back of my head from constantly lying on it. They told me my hair would grow back. *It better!* This was a minor issue though when compared to actual health problems due to lying prone for such a long time. For example, my blood pressure, like my muscles, had decreased due to inertia and me lying prone. My body had to learn to sit upright again. They had special wheelchairs for this "retraining." These chairs could be moved gradually from a flat/horizontal position to a seated position.

This retraining would take some time. It took a number of days of practice for me to finally achieve the ability to sit up at a forty-five-degree angle. At this stage, my nurse said, "Hey, let's go cruise around this wing of the hospital and see some new surroundings." The idea terrified me. This may sound surprising, but I did not want to go. I did not want to leave my room. My room had become my security blanket. In fact, I didn't even want to leave my bed.

But my nurse knew I had to take this step (no pun intended). My mom knew I had to take this step. After some convincing, they talked me into going just outside my door. I asked to pause there for a moment. Then I let them wheel me to the end of the hall. It was scary. But it was interesting too.

As I ventured out of my room, I could see other patients' rooms. *I wonder how they're doing. I wonder what their condition is.* It was also nice to travel down the hallway looking at pictures on the walls and seeing the nurses' station, anything that meant I didn't have to look at ceiling tiles! At the end of the hallway, there was a large window that looked out a different direction than the window in my room. It was much sunnier here, and the new view was stimulating for my mind. I squinted in the warm sunlight, since my eyes had grown accustomed to primarily indoor lighting. *I am ready to go back to my room, but I will take this "baby step" again tomorrow.*

While taking a welcomed nap one afternoon, I received an unexpected visit from my ER doctor. He still remembered me from my afternoon in the UCD Emergency Center three weeks ago. He reintroduced himself to my mom. Standing over my bed while I slept, he said to her, "I see a lot of people come into the ER with just a scratch, and they are screaming their heads off at everybody. But your son David, with the catastrophic injury that he had, was so polite. He was saying 'please' and 'thank you' and was asking permission for things. I was blown away. I just wanted to let you know how impressed I and many others are with your son."

With a tear trickling down her face, my mom simply said, "Thank you."

A new daily routine began to take shape for me there in the regular floor of the hospital. My day would begin with a nurse helping me with bathroom care and Ron helping me with range of motion stretches. Then I would get a sponge bath (not as exciting as you might think) and get my hair washed. The hair wash wasn't exciting either; it was a rinseless shampoo. Doesn't that sound horrible?

The only good part about my morning was breakfast. Being weaned off the tube feeding and getting to eat actual food had been a process. For a number of days, I had been allowed ice chips on my tongue when I got hot; that was so refreshing! Then we stepped it up a notch—pina colada popsicles! They were delicious! Finally, I was off the feeding tube and allowed actual food. It was the real stuff now!

After many weeks of tube feeding, it was so nice to taste and eat actual food. I even had a menu to choose from! For breakfast, there was scrambled eggs, bacon, sausage, pancakes, and more, and for lunch and dinner, I could choose a hamburger, chicken, fish, pasta, and so on. I even had scampi! And the food was honestly really good! I don't mean good for being hospital food; I mean really delicious! So my mornings now started off nicely with a yummy breakfast.

After breakfast, I had my usual x-rays and blood tests. They had a mobile x-ray machine that travelled to my room, which was very convenient. The daily blood tests were annoying, but I found a way around the pain of the needle. I learned that blood could be drawn from the back of the hand. I didn't have feeling on the back of my hand, so I would ask the phlebotomist to draw blood from there. I wouldn't tell them that I couldn't feel it though, because I didn't want them to not be careful and gentle. Sometimes, I would even wince as if I could feel it. Bad, huh?

Every afternoon included physical therapy. It was nothing too intense, just some wrist weights and strengthening exercises. The rest of my day was more of the same, except now I could have more visitors. This just brought more smiles to my face.

The evenings were the most relaxing time of the day. With most of the medical necessities finished earlier, my family and I could spend quality time together. While my mom was there in the hospital with me a majority of the time, my dad was also there often. One night, after he helped feed me dinner, he shared with me his experience after hearing the news of my accident. "Jonathan called me while waiting for the ambulance to arrive," he said, "and told me you had been injured."

"Did Jonathan know how injured I was?" I asked.

"He didn't give any details about your injury. I just assumed you had broken your arm or leg."

"So you didn't know I was paralyzed?"

"No. All I knew was that you were hurt. I jumped in my car and raced down to Lake of the Pines. But when I arrived at the gate and explained the emergency, the guard would not let me enter. I asked her if an ambulance had just driven by. She responded with, 'Are you a lawyer?'"

"What? No way!" I exclaimed.

"She did!" he continued. "She eventually let me enter. I picked up the boys, drove them home, and went to the hospital. I walked right into the ER and saw you lying on a gurney. After we chatted for a moment, a nurse led me to the nurses' station to talk to the doctor. A doctor approached me and bluntly said, 'I'm Dr. Pak. Your son has a broken neck.' It was the worst bedside manner I've ever experienced. I was stunned to the core by the devastating news. I went back to you and tried to say something comforting and encouraging, and then I drove right to the UC Davis Med Center. I was there waiting for you when you arrived in the helicopter."

"Wow!" I responded. "I had no idea about any of that."

Around the fourth week, a psychologist appeared at my bedside to help me cope with this traumatic change to my life. In an official, "by the book" manner, he listed for me the emotional stages that I would be going through. Anger and denial were the first two steps he listed.

In the moments when I hadn't been counting ceiling tiles in ICU, I had explored different emotions and reactions. Anger was one that I had thought about but had not actually felt. First of all, I had rarely ever gotten angry in my whole life, but that's beside the point. I realized that my current situation confronted me with an extraordinary challenge. Even if I wanted to be angry, there was no person I could be angry at for this accident. No one did me wrong or harmed me. I, personally, hadn't done something stupid or foolish. The only target left for my anger would be God. But that option never (and I mean *never*) entered my mind. *How can I be mad at God? He is God!*

Having been raised Christian and knowing the Bible, I firmly believed that God was in control of all things. If He allowed this to happen to me, He must have had a good reason. Besides, who am I to question God, the Creator and Almighty God? I just trusted Him and followed the old cliché, "Everything happens for a reason." In fact, when friends would visit me in the hospital, many tried to be uplifting and tell me that same cliché. I would kindly reply, "I know."

I knew, though, and believed that it was more than just a cliché. It was a promise. It comes from a Bible verse that I have clung to, now more than ever. Romans 8:28 states, "God causes all things to work together for good to those who love God, to those who are called according to His purpose."

How can I be angry at God when He has promised that, if I love Him, this horrible injury will work out for good. And when I say *good*, I don't mean good like I will be physically healed or will win the lottery. I mean—and that Bible verse means—that what God sees as good will happen. I believe this *good* probably has to do with things of an eternal perspective, like someone repenting of sinful ways or someone becoming a Christian and giving his/her life to Jesus. So, there on my hospital bed, not being able to move, I was hoping, praying, trusting, knowing that some good would happen because of this...that maybe one person would come to Jesus because of the faith, hope, and attitude I maintained.

The other stage the psychologist told me I would experience was denial. I hadn't gone through denial yet. I actually didn't see myself ever going through denial. That's probably denial right there. To be completely honest, I think I masked my denial under "positive thinking." I could grasp the fact that I had experienced a horrendous injury, but I also believed that I could overcome it and be physically whole again. The reality was, of course, that my injury was most likely permanent, as in lifelong. That's the part I didn't really focus on. But I liked to tell myself that I wasn't in denial.

This introspection led me back to the very moment of my accident. My first thought was, "Well, God will heal me." Looking back, I wondered if maybe that thought was denial of what had just happened to me. I preferred to believe that it was God comforting me. Either way, it had given me peace and kept me calm in a very trying time (though I wouldn't mind it if God healed me anyway).

I believed, and still do, without a doubt, that God can heal me. I also believed, and still do, that scientists will discover a cure for paralysis in my lifetime. I don't think that's denial.

Another aspect of the psychological counseling that the hospital felt was necessary for new SCI patients was to send in a peer, a young man in a wheelchair, to talk to me and assist me in the coping process. I actually didn't feel like I really needed help coping, but I also figured it wouldn't hurt to hear what he had to say. *I'm sure he's a nice guy,* I thought. I assumed that he was going to provide encouragement and comfort—as well as useful information.

He was wheeled into my room by a nurse, who parked him near my bed and then left us alone. He was young, early twenties. We introduced ourselves. Our initial conversation was short but polite. It wasn't long before he said to me, "This accident has been the worst thing ever in my life." *Understandable.* "My life now is awful. All of my friends have left me, and now the only people who spend time with me are my nurses."

Wow. This poor guy. How sad. I really feel bad for this guy. I need to try to cheer him up. So there I was, flat on my back in a hospital bed, and I said to him, "Hey, it will be okay. These things will all get better. It just takes faith." Yes, I could see the irony of the situation.

He didn't say much after that. A few minutes later, the nurse came back in and wheeled him out. *Wow! How did the hospital ever choose that guy to console and encourage anybody?!*

I made a major decision for my life after that conversation. *I never want to be a bummer. I never want to be so down that people will not want to hang out with me.*

I hope I don't lose my friends.

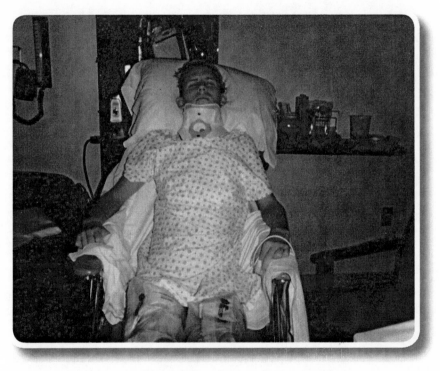

Sitting up in my hospital room.

CHAPTER 7

After six weeks at UC Davis Medical Center, my health finally improved to the point where I no longer needed to be in a hospital. It was now time for me to leave this temporary home, hoping never to return. *Finally! This was certainly good news!* However, my next "home" was not yet the familiar house that I had grown up in. My next home was the next step in my recovery—a physical rehabilitation center.

As much as I was done with hospitals and just wanted to go home, I knew this stage was extremely important if I were going to live with a severe disability. The rehab center would push me physically to develop what muscles I had use of in order to become as independent as possible. I was told I would also learn exactly what my needs were and how to instruct a caregiver to help me with those needs. With all that said, I was scared to leave the hospital—just as I had been scared to leave my hospital room. *What if I have some severe emergency? What if I have trouble breathing? There are doctors and nurses and equipment right here! Ugh! Wow, this is going to be a lot of work.*

But as soon as those thoughts ran through my mind, another thought bubbled to the surface: *I'm ready to do what I have to do.* I didn't just want to live; I wanted a life.

There were a number of rehab centers to choose from. My mom, dad, and father researched many facilities and even visited a few. The best rehab hospital was Craig Hospital in Colorado. It was expensive, but it was a top-notch facility specializing in spinal cord injuries. Rancho Los Amigos in Los Angeles County was also a very well-known rehab hospital, with an established history of cutting-edge therapies. However, after my parents' visit there, they described it as old and institution like. They also visited Shriners Hospital in San Francisco. This hospital was for children only, and its services were free. My parents wanted me to be the one to decide where I would go. Cost was not a factor because insurance would cover it.

This was a big decision. It could affect the rest of my life. If one hospital was more aggressive in its physical therapy program, perhaps I could gain mobility or skills that I wouldn't at a different hospital. Also, being near family and friends could be a valuable support for me emotionally. Although Craig Hospital was one of the best rehab hospitals in the United States for spinal cord injuries and Rancho Los Amigos was well respected, I felt that being close to friends and family was more important. I chose to get my physical rehabilitation at Shiners Hospital. It sounded more personal, friendly, and homey, and I really liked that visitors would be able to see me more often. An additional reason I chose Shriners is because my mom's neighbors, who were Shriners, told her that they would be sure to get me into the twelve-patient facility.

It was late in the evening a number of days later when I was transported by ambulance from the UC Davis Med Center to Shriners Hospital. It was about a two-hour drive. My mom and dad followed me down. I arrived to a dimly lit, rundown-looking, old two-story building. *That* was not a good first impression. I was wheeled inside on a gurney and was surprised and happy to be greeted by a very attractive, blonde woman. I'm not implying that Shriners Hospital intentionally plans to welcome all its new patients this way; I just think I lucked out. *That* was a good first impression!

A night-shift nurse assisted me into bed, and my dad drove back home, leaving me and my mom to chat briefly before I went to sleep. While she was talking about her first impressions of this place and the drive down here, my heart was breaking over a profound yet simple question I had been pondering. I couldn't keep it to myself any longer. I blurted out, "Mom, why didn't I just walk into the lake? Why did I have to dive in?" It all came down to that one question. That one factor changed everything, caused all of this. My mom comforted me, and I knew in my heart that God was in control. *But, still, that one factor was just so simple and yet so devastating!*

The next morning, I met my primary nurse. I was really hoping my nurse would be the blonde woman I had met the previous night, but sadly, it was not her. I was assigned a male nurse, John. By this time, with all my hospital experience, my conservative ways had learned that there were many good male nurses in the field. John began to teach me the process of what I had to do to get up and ready for the day. Not having the use of my arms, legs, and even hands and fingers, I required help with pretty much every aspect of daily personal care. He helped me with range of motion for my arms and legs and taught me additional stretches that I had not learned at UC Davis Med Center.

John also helped me with breakfast, bathroom care, bathing, and getting dressed. I've got to say that I was a very modest person who appreciated my privacy in personal matters. However, God must have intervened, thankfully, for I acquired the acceptance that it was now just a fact of life that I needed help with these personal duties. I imagine that this would be a huge hurdle for many patients.

I hadn't gotten dressed in clothes since I dressed myself the morning of my accident. I had been in hospital gowns ever since. Shriners Hospital did not allow their patients to wear hospital gowns, so they had instructed my mom to purchase clothes and shoes for me that were conducive to exercising.

This process of just getting up and ready for the day took about two and a half hours. I was learning that most things in my life now, if done correctly, would take much longer than they used to before my accident. So much of my day was taken up by my care. Out of a number of negative effects of my accident, this would be one of my bigger frustrations.

I've got to remind myself to be thankful of the fact that at least I'm getting up. I've got to stay positive!

Now that I was *up* in my wheelchair (I use the word *up* loosely, for I physically still could not sit completely upright) and my privacy curtain was opened, I could see that I was in a large room with high ceilings and great big windows. The sun shone brightly through the windows and reflected off the tile floor. Four other teenage boys shared my room. I could see them also being assisted into their wheelchairs.

Tom was from Texas; he seemed a bit wild and crazy. And yes, he wore a cowboy hat, a worn, old cowboy hat.

Phillipe, Estaban, and Raul were from Mexico, as Shriners Hospital brought up many patients from Mexico who were in need of good physical rehabilitation. These three didn't speak any English. I was told that Phillipe had been a physically normal kid who woke up one day from a nap and was completely paralyzed. That's crazy! And sad. I guess he had picked up some sort of virus. Estaban was the quiet one. Raul was physically immense. His favorite thing to say during physical therapy was, "No puedo," which means "I can't!" No Puedo became his nickname.

While John helped me with my morning routine, my mom drove to Grass Valley to get my brothers and bring them back down to the hospital. They arrived that afternoon, and all of us were given an introductory tour of my new "home." We were informed that Shriners Hospital focused on getting its patients back to "normal" life. Their philosophy was that we, the patients, were not "sick" and no longer in a "hospital. That meant that we would be bathed and dressed every day, that we would strengthen and develop our muscles in physical therapy, relearn how to do various daily living activities, have fun, eat meals in a dining room, and go on outings. *I like the sound of all of that!*

I also met another patient, Liane. She was quadriplegic as a result of a car accident. After talking for a bit, it was clear to both of us that we had a lot in common. We were about the same age, we both had a positive attitude, we both were honor students and campus leaders in high school, and we both had a good sense of humor. The two of us quickly became good friends. I think we were good therapy for each other, for we could talk with each other, share our frustrations, and understand what the other was feeling and experiencing.

That evening, my mom, brothers, and I ate dinner together in the dining room, and after my night nurse got me ready for bed, they closed my privacy curtain, huddled around my bed, and watched *Little Shop of Horrors* with me. Dinner and a movie became our ritual for about two weeks while my family stayed in a guest room until returning home. It was such a comfort for me to have them there. I know they felt blessed to be there, and I'm sure my brothers didn't mind the hospital's game room and video arcade.

The next morning, I got a glimpse of my next three months. After my normal morning routine, my first task of the day was physical therapy. John wheeled me out of my room and down the hall. After passing the dining room and game room, we turned into the physical therapy room. It was a very large room with exercise tables, mats, and various equipment, not to mention a number of therapists and patients.

My physical therapist was a young woman named Susan. She was personable and had experience in helping people with spinal cord injuries. On my first day, we got acquainted with each other, and she tested my strength and what muscles I had use of. Similar to my level of sensation, I could not use any muscles chest down. I could use my shoulders and my biceps, and that was pretty much it. With strengthening exercises, there was a chance I would be able to do a number of activities though. There were certain skills she wanted me to try—balancing while sitting, pushing my own wheelchair, and transferring myself from my wheelchair to my bed. It was hard to imagine that those skills would even be possible.

I have a lot of work ahead of me these next few months.

After movie time that night with my dad and brothers, I was exhausted but did not fall asleep right away. As I lay on my side, staring at the privacy curtain around my bed and dwelling on this devastating and all-consuming injury of mine, I could not shake a persistent thought.

How did this happen to me? How did this happen to David Kline? He is the outgoing, athletic, social one. This isn't him. This can't be right. This kind of thing happens to someone else. This doesn't happen to David Kline.

The overwhelming shock of this thought brought me to the verge of tears. This thought had popped into my mind before. It wasn't an angry thought. It wasn't a "mad at God" thought. It was just a thought that caught me off guard when I would suddenly think about where and who I was at that moment compared to where and who I used to be. I let out a quiet sigh. I forced myself to thank God for what blessings I had and what promises He had made.

Plus, it could always be worse. I sighed again. *I just have to keep goin'.*

My early days at Shriners Hospital involved some basic and necessary steps. I first needed to be fitted for custom arm braces, which I would soon be wearing each night while I slept. Over the last two months, my arms had gotten so tight that they could not be straightened all the way. These braces would hopefully rectify this problem. Also, after much practice, I was finally able to sit completely upright in my wheelchair without passing out. That's something! Unfortunately, though, now that I was sitting upright and tall, I discovered that my upper-body strength and balance was incredibly weak. It was so weak that I had to have a very uncomfortable strap tied around my chest and to the back of my wheelchair just to prevent me from falling forward.

I was working very hard in physical therapy, but I was not progressing in most of my physical therapy goals. Although I quickly learned how to control a motorized wheelchair, my physical therapist wanted me to learn how to push my own manual wheelchair. Because I do not have the use of my fingers and am thus not able to grab the wheels, I was placed in a lightweight manual chair that had pegs attached to the wheels that I could push with my palms. These pegs were hard for me to reach because of the chest strap holding me back, and when I did lean forward far enough to reach down to the pegs, it took an enormous amount of effort for me to sit back upright.

Add that to the physical exertion required to push the chair the slightest distance, and I was exhausted! I was not able to go very far pushing my wheelchair. The hallway outside the therapy room was my practice area. It was a looong hallway with smooth tile floors (good for wheelchairs). With my current limited strength level and skill, I would not be able to control this chair on any kind of real-world terrain that had even the slightest upslope or downslope.

I don't see how I can have an independent life in a chair like this.

For most of my days at Shriners, excluding this practice time, I got around using my motorized wheelchair.

I had even less success in my sitting balance and transferring. *Transferring* is the term used to describe how a patient gets in and out of a wheelchair. To practice these skills, my physical therapist would first put me on one of the low padded tables used for stretching. Some of the bigger and heavier patients would be transferred from chair to table or vice versa using a Hoyer lift, a large mechanical contraption that uses a sling to pick up a patient.

For me, my therapist would do a pivot transfer. She would lean down toward me, pinch my knees between her knees, lean my upper body over her back, and lift and pivot my body and set me down on the table. Then she would swing my legs over the edge of the table and sit up my upper body, making sure to hold me and keep me from falling over.

The goal was for me to prop myself up with my arms behind me, scoot myself to the very edge of the table, somehow pull my wheelchair close, and then transfer myself to my chair. I didn't see how I could ever do it. I had been working on this for weeks already and still couldn't even hold myself up.

How am I going to do the other, even harder steps? How can I sit up from a lying-down position when I can barely lift my head up off the table?

I just didn't have the strength to do those skills, which are so important for my independence. This was frustrating, very frustrating. I had been so accustomed to success before my accident. I could put my mind and effort to anything, and I would achieve the results I wanted. But not now.

I was also struggling in my occupational therapy (OT). OT includes nonmedical skills required for work, school, or just daily living. One area that my occupational therapist was trying to help me with was handwriting. I could not move my fingers at all and could barely move my arms. Because my wrists were so weak, I wore braces that wrapped around each hand and Velcroed six inches up each arm. My therapist would attach to this brace a small splint that held a pen. After rolling my motorized chair up to a raised table, I would try to write on pads of paper that had been clamped down to the table. My writing was not very good, and I was not seeing much improvement after all my practicing. I tried typing on a computer as well. I used the same brace, but my therapist placed an eraser on the tip of the pen for typing. This was an easier skill than writing but would still require lots of practice. *Even if I get good at typing, it's still just one key at a time. Wow!*

An even more important skill that I could not do was feeding myself. This whole time, nurses, family, or friends had been feeding me. It seemed like everyone had his or her own preferred bite size and preferred pace of eating. I was always having to say, "Smaller bites, please" or "Slow down, please" or "I'm ready." This was a little frustrating. I never made an issue of it, for I knew that they were just trying to help me out.

To assist me in feeding myself, the hand brace that I wore came equipped with a leather pocket or slit, in which a fork or spoon could be inserted. If I was lucky enough to scoop or stab some food on my plate, the problem then was that I just couldn't get my hand up to my mouth. To resolve this problem, my therapist then hooked up a metal contraption that clamped to the armrest of my wheel-chair. My arm rested in a "cradle," and when I would push my elbow down to the floor, the cradle would tilt upward, bringing my hand and fork up to my mouth. At least, that was the theory. When I would try it, my hand would come up, but it would also rotate out to my side. I would watch my food come up and then curve away. *I guess I could feed a person sitting next to me really well.* My therapist eventually abandoned this idea.

There was still another area of physical therapy that my therapist had me work on. It was called the tilt table, or standing frame. It was nice because I didn't have to do anything. That sounds really lazy of me! First, I was transferred to the table. Next, I was strapped tightly to the table at the knees, waist, and chest. At this point, I was ready, and we pushed the button to slowly tilt the table. With my feet flat against the foot rest, the table was tilted up. We went very slowly, a few degrees at a time. A lofty goal for any SCI patient would be to tilt the table all the way so that the patient would be "standing" straight up and down. This takes a lot of time and practice and acclimation, for an SCI patient has weaker leg bones and weaker blood pressure due to not standing up. Therefore, standing on a tilt table can strengthen bones and blood pressure and can also improve circulation and kidney health. After a few tries, I got halfway to standing up, about forty-five degrees. I knew I would have to keep practicing this one too.

Despite my lack of success in the goals set by my therapists, there were positive aspects to my rehabilitation, and glimmers of returning to a "normal" life were surfacing. Back home, school was back in session for the fall, and I was still a student who needed to continue his education. With all that I had been through and was going through, it was easy to forget that I was a high school senior now who had schoolwork to do.

While discussing this on the phone with my mom, we agreed that she would ask my high school back home to mail my books to me. To our surprise, my home/hospital teacher from my high school drove down to San Francisco with my books so that he could meet me and be able to report back to everyone at school how I was doing. And so, with his visit, I added English, economics, and history to my daily routine.

I also had a school-related duty that I needed to perform, whether I was physically at the school or not. At the end of my junior year, my peers had voted me to be their senior class vice president and my best friend, Erik, to be their senior class president. Now that we were in our senior year, we were required to participate in weekly student council meetings at the high school.

I was able to "attend," thanks to an electronics company in my hometown. They had invented a phone that could transmit still photos to a similar phone. This company gave one phone to the school and one to me down at Shriners Hospital. So each week during the meeting, I sat in front of my phone, listening to the discussion and viewing photos of the students at the meeting. This was a welcome joy for me. To be honest though, I really didn't pay attention to the meetings. I spent most of the meetings taking goofy pictures of myself and listening for the chuckles as each student passed the phone around the table and saw my silly faces.

On the weekends, my friends drove down (about two and a half hours) to see me. It was always a thrill to spend time with them and laugh like the old days. They would tell me all the gossip back home and relay greetings and well wishes from friends who couldn't make the drive down. I missed home. I missed having my life. I missed being part of the action at my school. It was weird to think that everyone's life back home was going on as normal.

It was also difficult though for my closest friends— Scott, Erik, Steve, and Darren. With the goal of trying to physically and emotionally deal with my injury, they wrote, filmed, and edited a movie for me as a way to express their emotions regarding my accident. I think, most of all, they wanted to express their love for me. It was some time later that I got to see it, but just knowing that they were working on it for me meant everything to me. By the way, the movie (a collection of sketches) was both poignant and hilarious, including an interview with God about my accident and a scene from Sesame Street. *I've got great friends!*

More thoughtfulness was heading my way. During a phone call with my mom, she informed me that my soccer coach from Nevada Union, Coach Crowe, contacted my former coach from Forest Lake, Coach Kopec, and asked him if he would be interested in a soccer game in tribute of me. "This Friday night," my mom told me, "in the Nevada Union football stadium, your current soccer team will be playing your former soccer team in a game in your honor." She was so excited to tell me this news! I was thrilled too!

The turnout for the game was huge, and both teams had a great time. During halftime, I was called on the phone at the hospital and my voice was patched into the stadium loudspeakers so that I could say hi and thank those in attendance. Even though I wasn't there, that moment of generosity sure made me feel appreciated.

Another very touching moment was when three female friends—Rena, Amber, and Keslie—drove down from Grass Valley on homecoming night to have dinner with me. They had prepared a delicious meal with all the fixings. At the hospital, we were allowed to use a private conference room where the girls set the table, including polished silverware, linen tablecloth, and candles. Their kindness was so thoughtful and sweet. It made my day.

Yes, I have to admit, I did have some good times at Shriners'. In fact, some of the fun was planned and considered to be part of Shriners' rehabilitation program. Liane, two other patients, and I were taken to a baseball game to watch the San Francisco Giants play. I'm sure the purpose of the trip wasn't just for us to have fun; it probably was also intended that we freshly injured folk get used to maneuvering our wheelchairs in a crowd and also just mentally get used to being in a wheelchair out in public. We had a great time at the game surrounded by thousands of drunk Giants fans. And it actually wasn't too bad having to "function" in a crowd and deal with uneven sidewalks and bumpy surfaces.

We were also taken out to a restaurant for pizza a couple times. Oh my goodness, pizza! This was so much better than hospital pizza! It was great to get out and participate in normal everyday activities. Shelley joined us one evening for dinner while she was visiting from college. Boy oh boy, was it a treat to spend time with her!

Now that we patients were reminded what great food tasted like, we started having family members order pizza from the restaurant and bring it back to the hospital. Sometimes, when my mom spent the night at Shriners Hospital, she would make pancakes for breakfast for me and Liane. Or if Liane's parents and family brought a big dinner, I would join them in the meeting hall for a private dinner. So I guess being in a rehab hospital wasn't all that bad.

Another part of my positive experience at Shriners was my primary nurse, John. He sincerely tried to make me feel at home and feel like my life could return to some resemblance of normal. He went out of his way to help me in this endeavor by asking me about my life and interests and habits before I became paralyzed. One day, I happened to mention to him that before my accident, in order to manage my teenage acne, I put on a blue clay face mask almost every night. I know that must shatter my macho, tough-guy image! The next evening, while John was helping me get ready for bed, he opened up a bag and pulled out a jar of a similar blue clay! "Ta-da!" he exclaimed.

"John! Thank you!" I responded. "You are so thoughtful!"

He washed my face and then applied the mask just like I used to. As we waited for it to dry, he had to, of course, tease me a bit! I'm sure it was quite a sight—me with a blue face sitting up in bed in Shriners Hospital. Fortunately, my privacy curtain was closed. Within fifteen minutes, I could feel the familiar sensation of the mask drying and tightening on my face. For that moment, life seemed normal. Sometimes it just takes the little things to make a difference!

I received a fantastic surprise in the middle of October—Shriners Hospital was letting me go home for the weekend for my birthday! I was so excited! It was two weeks away, and my mom, also very excited, got right to work on all the preparations. One of her grand plans was to arrange a huge get-together with hundreds of my friends—yes, hundreds.

She talked with the school near her house regarding the use of their gymnasium and reserved a couple of school busses to get people there. This was turning into a big deal. I was looking forward to it, but I was definitely not as excited as my mom. In fact, by the time that weekend arrived, I was feeling too overwhelmed by the thought of so much attention. I wasn't ready for it. My mom understood my apprehension and cancelled the event. I was relieved. After spending so much time isolated in hospital rooms, I knew that I was not mentally ready for such an event and so much attention. I also knew that this hesitancy and shyness was a departure from who I was before my accident.

I did, though, still spend some time with close friends on my birthday. We went out to the Empire Mine State Park so that I could see some old, familiar sights. It was a very bumpy ride over the gravel roads, but at the same time, it was so wonderful to be with my best friends and to be outside in the woods. This was the first time since my accident that I got to do anything like this.

One other reminder of my life and home that occurred that weekend was when my dad carried me up the stairs at our house so that I could see my old room. Although he had already boxed up my things, knowing that I wouldn't be using that room anymore, it was very poignant and special for me to see my room. Overall, this trip home was great for my spirits as it was a reminder that I had a life to return to.

Following that fantastic trip home and throughout my time at Shriners Hospital, there were constant questions from my family and friends and me as to when I could be done there and go home for good. Initially, January had been mentioned as a possibility. I was hoping for sooner. As November ended and my health and recovery strengthened, my hopes for a release date that would allow me to be home for Christmas really began to blossom. Finally, after many days of anticipation, I was given word that I could go home on December 18. I was so excited!

There was one final requirement that Shriners Hospital demanded before I could be discharged. My parents had to prove that they could take care of me for twenty-four hours on their own. My mom accepted the challenge, and we moved into the hospital's "apartment" for twenty-four hours. We hung out and played games. When I needed any physical care, I instructed my mom in how to help, just as I had been taught to do by my nurses and therapists.

That night, as we were lying in our beds, in the dark and the quiet, I suddenly said to my mom, "I'm not going to go to college." I wasn't sure I was ready to go. This whole disability thing was just too new for me, and I felt uneasy, unsure, and a little scared about my future.

My mom got out of her bed, walked over to mine, and then calmly replied, "David, you're eighteen now. You can make your own decisions. I've never had to tell you what friends you can hang out with or what places you can go to. You've always made good choices. But, David, you *will* go to college."

That was the extent of our conversation that night. She knew what I hadn't realized: if I was going to make it through this life with a disability, I would have to have an education. I would have to overcome my doubts and fears. This would be a big step for me, an important step. The next morning, while my mom was helping me get up, I told her, "Mom, I was really sad last night. And, Mom, I will go to college."

Her smile said it all.

I received some great news a few days before I left Shriners. My grandmother (whom I called Nana) had arranged a gift for me. My mom's mom was the godliest person I knew. She always prayed with us, quoted Bible verses to us, and asked how our walk with God was going. She was kind, sweet, and gentle. Nana was well into her eighties. She had recently willingly relinquished her driver's license. She had been "the little old lady from Pasadena" in her big blue Cadillac. Well, she knew I would need a vehicle. No, she didn't give me the Cadillac, but she generously bought me a wheelchair-accessible van! I was so excited!

I had assumed that I would have to be physically picked up out of my wheelchair and transferred to the front passenger seat of a car every time I went somewhere. That would have been such a hassle and such a strain on whoever was helping me. The van Nana got me was a minivan with a small ramp at the side sliding door. The front passenger seat had been removed, so I could be pushed up the ramp and parked in the front passenger space. This would be so much easier and quicker! *Thank you, Nana!*

My final day at Shriners Hospital was filled with goodbyes and hugs. I was especially sad to say goodbye to Liane and John, but I knew we would always stay in touch. It had been 114 days since I got to Shriners Hospital and 164 days total since my accident. That's a long time to be away from home, especially when it wasn't planned. I was melancholy as I reflected back on those 164 days, how much time that's been, and all that I've been through. I was disappointed that I didn't reach many of the goals set for me by my physical therapist and occupational therapist.

I still can't feed myself. I still can't push myself in a manual chair. I still can't transfer myself. I did improve some, but

I wonder if my therapists should've pushed me harder. Did I even have the potential and ability in the first place to reach these goals? I'm not a quitter. Am I?

Many thoughts filled my head. At the same time, I was very excited! I was going home and going to be home for Christmas! I was going home for good!

Dan, Randy, Steve, and Scott visiting me during
my first days at Shriners Hospital.

Liane and I and a nurse in the dining room at Shriners Hospital.

A fantastic Homecoming dinner with Rena, Keslie, and Amber!

A visit from Shelley at Shriners Hospital.

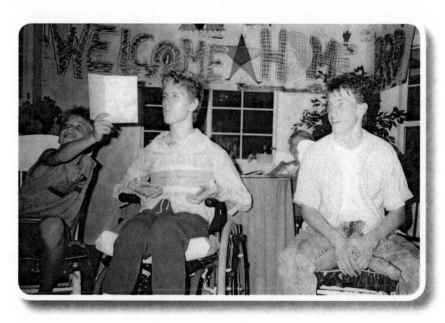

Jonathan and Steve join other family and
friends for my birthday visit home.

THE WHITE HOUSE
WASHINGTON

Santa Barbara

August 31, 1987

Dear David:

I've just learned about your accident from your father.

I know this must be an especially difficult time for you, and I just want you to know that I'm rooting for you. While you may find yourself feeling low in spirits at times, I'm sure you realize there are a great many people who care about you and who are eager to help you through this time of struggle. My advice is -- when people want to help you, let them. When you get to be my age, you realize that no one makes it without a lot of help from others. Remember that life is full of possibilities, and some of the greatest men and women of history have been those who overcame adversity through courage and perseverance.

May God bless you and keep you.

Sincerely,

Ronald Reagan

Mr. David Kline
Shriners Children's Hospital-SCIU
1701 19th Avenue
San Francisco, California 94122

Receiving these encouraging words from the President of the United States was such an honor!

CHAPTER 8

My mom picked me up from Shriners Hospital in my new van. What a blessing to have that van! We left Shriners and headed home.

I didn't get to go "home" home, for I went to my mom's new house, about twenty minutes away from where I grew up. Her house was one level and had a bedroom that I could stay in. My mom also had found a caregiver/attendant to help me. Her name was Neville; she would be my first caregiver.

Neville greeted me at the door when I arrived. That first day home, I could see that she was thoughtful, kind, and caring. Her experience as a caregiver and her willingness to listen to my specific needs were also quite evident. I told her about the care and routine I was accustomed to, as Shriners Hospital had taught me to, and she listened and followed directions perfectly. She assisted me with my morning routine as well as helping me with my care during other times of the day. With Neville's easygoing temperament and compassionate caregiving, the physical aspect of my return couldn't have gone any better, and the transition from rehab facility to home was smooth because of her.

Being back near home and with family and friends was wonderful. There was a steady flow of visitors to welcome me home. Some of these friends and acquaintances had not seen me since my accident. I'm sure it was difficult for them, observing the very drastic change in my physical appearance from my former active and athletic body and my outgoingness to my now weak appearance in a wheelchair. My positive attitude and humor hadn't changed though, and I quickly put my visitors at ease. We talked and laughed about shared memories from the past and about the things we had each been up to over the last five months.

When around friends and visitors, I made a mental decision for myself. I decided that I would not complain or pout or be "down" around my friends, for I figured, "Who would want to hang out with someone like that?" I just didn't want to be a downer; I didn't want people to not want to spend time with me.

I was always positive on the outside when interacting with others. I didn't have to act, for this positive outlook was pretty genuine, not phony. And I was honestly positive on the inside too. However, not far down below the surface, I really, really wanted to walk again.

This was a recurring topic in my thoughts. I began to pray each night, "Lord, I pray that tomorrow would be the day that you heal me." In addition to my prayers for family and friends, I would say that prayer every night as I fell asleep in the hope that it would come true.

When I left Shriners Hospital and came home, I made a decision to stop using my motorized wheelchair and to use my manual wheelchair instead. I had used a motorized wheelchair almost exclusively while at Shriners Hospital. I still could not push myself in the manual chair, so that meant I needed someone to push my chair wherever I needed to go.

Some may wonder why I would make this decision. One reason is that the manual chair weighed much, much less than the motorized chair, so it was much easier for friends to get me and my chair up a few stairs and to other difficult places. But the real reason, to be honest, was that the motorized wheelchair looked too "disabled" and too "*permanently* disabled." Being so big and so bulky, the motorized wheelchair made my disability look very serious and very permanent. I was too self-conscious, and I was also still hoping that I would be walking soon. I think my decision was based on my perception of how others saw me and my perception of how I saw myself.

This brings up a psychological and emotional subject for me. I did not want to appear vulnerable. I was adamant about that.

The truth, of which I am quite aware, is that I am vulnerable. I am weak. I am limited. I do have insecurities.

I didn't want others to notice that or to think that about me. But I suppose they did.

After a wonderful Christmas, January came around, and it was time for me to go back to school. This was my senior year of high school! Obviously, it was not going the way I had planned, but I was excited to see so many friends whom I hadn't seen for so long and to get to see my best friends every day. In preparation for my return, my high school academic counselor asked my mom if she thought I should be placed in special education classes and/or be granted extra time for my homework and easier requirements for my assignments. My mom obviously replied, "No way! There's nothing wrong with his brain!"

Another area of preparation was for me to make arrangements for my health and physical well-being while at school. People who sit in wheelchairs must be diligent to take care of their bottoms to not get pressure sores from sitting all day. For that reason, I had been taught at Shriners Hospital that I had to tilt my wheelchair way back every two hours for ten to fifteen minutes at a time to take the pressure off and give my skinny bottom a break. I was very disciplined about this.

It meant I always had to keep an eye on the clock. It also meant that I had to plan and arrange for someone to help tilt back my chair every two hours. At home, someone could set a stack of pillows on an armchair or couch and then tilt my chair back onto it. At school or out and about, there was not a soft stack of pillows, so whomever I was with would sit in a chair and tilt my wheelchair back onto him/her so that my head rested on his/her shoulder. Sure, we would get looks from strangers, but it was something that had to be done. Besides, I never would complain when a really cute girl would tilt my chair back and rest my head on her shoulder. With that said, I arranged for help at school from friends and favorite teachers.

On my first day back to school, I got all bundled up due to the crisp, cold air. I waited inside the house, listening for the honk from the school bus. It came, right on time, and my mom opened our front door and wheeled me to the bus at the edge of our driveway.

It was a small bus. It was a "special" bus. I knew it would be. I needed a bus with a wheelchair lift and space for my chair inside. The driver loaded me into the bus and strapped my chair down securely. My mom waved good-bye. I was the only passenger. The ride was cold and bumpy in the back of that little bus. I couldn't help thinking how strange it was that "David Kline" needed to ride in one of those busses. I tried not to dwell on my changed circumstances, but to be honest, it was a strange feeling to be arriving at school in that bus and in a wheelchair, knowing that the last time I had been at this school I had been a popular star athlete and had driven myself there.

Oh, well. Life must go on. I'm back at school now!

My friend Steve met me at the front of the school as I was unloaded from the little bus. He greeted me with a smile and pushed me to my first class of the day, choir. I had been singing in choirs all my life, and it was a joy for me to be singing again and participating again in a choir, despite my now limited lung capacity. From choir, my friend Scott wheeled me to Speech and Debate, an extremely enter-taining class. It was also great fun going down the crowded halls, seeing friends' smiles and receiving friendly pats on the shoulder. Everyone was so welcoming and caring and happy to see me!

The rest of my school day was filled with English and psychology. I welcomed the mental stimulation and the educational challenge that school provided. I even told my psychology teacher, Mr. Stanley, to "treat me like any other student." I think he was surprised, but he agreed.

My first day back was great, and of course, my mom wanted to hear about every little detail when I got home.

Being back at school meant that I had homework to do each night. This posed some challenges. Though my brain worked just fine, physically I could not use my fingers and hands and could barely move my arms. With continued therapy and practice, my arm strength and dexterity had been improving, but I still could not write or type well enough.

To help me get through the school year, my mom handwrote all my assignments for me. For these essays and other homework, I would think quietly for a minute, put a few sentences together in my head, remember them, and then tell my mom what to write down. Phew! What a mental challenge that was! My mom continued to be such a great help to me!

Just as I was getting settled back into school and into a "normal" life, I was forced to face an issue that seriously affects just about every person with a spinal cord injury. The issue is skin breakdown, also known as pressure sores, also known as decubitus ulcers, also known as the plague of paralysis. For those of us in wheelchairs or for those who are bedridden, prevention is an ongoing challenge.

In my case, this meant diligently tilting my wheelchair every two hours. I had been doing that faithfully. But even with that focus, one night, after getting into bed and getting undressed, Neville noticed a little sore on my bottom. I think the sore formed because Neville hadn't noticed a pink pressure spot occurring daily and because I, being new to this disability thing, did not insist that she, my caregiver, check for pink spots on my skin (the first stage of skin breakdown) every day. *Bummer!*

I knew the only way my bottom could get better was for me to stay off it, meaning I could not get up in my chair and I must stay in bed resting on my side. Untreated pressure sores could become life-threatening, so the freedom I had of being in my chair and going to school and visiting friends came to a screeching halt until the pressure sore healed. That night, I mentally prepared myself for a few days stuck in bed to heal.

Three days came and went, and no noticeable healing had taken place. *What?! Why not?! This is awful!*

On a house call, my doctor explained that pressure sores develop under the skin from too much pressure and can require days, even weeks, to fully heal. To ease my worry, he also said that he had seen much, much worse pressure sores.

Well, that's good, I guess. "When will it get better? When can I get up?" I asked him.

"It's hard to say," he replied. "Keep off it, just like you're doing already."

Well, I want to be better. I want to get back to school and to life. I guess I just have to rest and give it more time.

After a few more days of rest, Neville noticed a slight improvement, but it certainly was not enough for me to be able to get up. We figured another week in bed should be enough time. *Ugh!* My mom called my school counselor asking for my assignments I'd already missed, plus all the upcoming work as well.

That second week came and went, and that annoying sore still hadn't healed enough. I'd be a fool to risk wasting two weeks of the bed rest I'd already invested, so again, coming to grips with the "joy" of paralysis, I had no other option but to stay put for another week. I was slowly beginning to realize that I must be a slow healer now due to the fact that I'm not up and moving and walking and generating good blood flow. Even so, I had a hard time hearing Neville report after three weeks of being confined to my bed, "David, you maybe need one more week."

Unbelievable! I've lost so much time already! Grrr. Fine, I can do another week! God, please help me get all better!

Of course, that was not the first time I had prayed over those last few weeks. Even though I was not getting better as fast as I hoped and prayed I would, I still wanted to bring my requests to God. And during that challenging time, I believed that God led me to the understanding that maybe He allowed me to suffer so that I could be an example to others. Not that I was more special, but that my acceptance and patience would prove how God can provide strength, peace, and faith during times of struggle. So for that reason, and because of my natural inclination to be positive, I tried to remain upbeat throughout this ordeal.

While I was restricted to bed rest and having to deal with the resulting emotional aspects, my brother Jonathan was having emotional troubles of his own. My mom informed me that he still struggled to cope with my accident and with the high probability that I would be disabled for the rest of my life. Focused on my own struggles, I was unaware of his heartache.

Fortunately, he confided in my mom his emotions. He revealed even more to her. What I didn't know, until many years later, was that he felt responsible for my accident. I would have wept like a baby if I had known he felt guilty about my accident. I knew, without a doubt, that it was a freak accident and that no one was to blame. How sad that he would take all of that on as his fault!

As any mom would be, my mom was devastated to hear that he felt that way. She knew she had to do something to help him overcome those feelings or, at least, alleviate this guilt. Knowing that government agencies often honor local heroes, she contacted Nevada County officials with the proposal that they honor Jonathan Kline for saving my life. She hoped that an award like that could boost his spirits. The Nevada County Board of Supervisors voted on the issue and approved the resolution!

Jonathan and my mom were invited to the next meeting for the presentation. At the beginning of the meeting, the secretary announced the first order of business: the Resolution of Commendation to Jonathan Kline. My little brother was called up in front of the board and those attending the meeting.

A board member shook Jonathan's hand, handed him the framed resolution, and read it aloud. Step by step, the resolution listed every action that Jonathan took that saved my life that day. The resolution ended with the proclamation, "Now, therefore, be it resolved by the County of Nevada acting by and through its Board of Supervisors that said Board does hereby express its admiration and appreciation to Jon Kline for his rescue of David Kline. The entire meeting hall erupted in applause. My mom still recalls how overwhelmed Jonathan looked to be a county hero! I wished I could have been there to see it! To this day, my brother still has that framed resolution.

Finally, after a month in bed, Neville declared the pressure sore healed, and I was able to get up! *Thank you, God! That was a grueling month!* That frustrating month stuck in bed away from friends and school was just an introduction to trying to live a normal life as a quadriplegic. One thing was becoming painfully evident: this would not be an easy life.

Getting back on that little, yellow school bus was good news as I went back to school. What a thrill it was when my friends and teachers welcomed me back! Of course, Mr. Stanley, my psychology teacher, took this special opportunity to remind me of what I had told him on that first day. In other words, I still had to complete all my missing work, which I did.

Just like any typical teenage boy, I wanted to have fun! I came up with a pretty clever idea one fine day, inspired by Jonathan and Adam's friend Tim, a Boy Scout. Tim came over and wanted us to help him earn his next badge. The Boy Scout manual required him to be blindfolded to see what it feels like to be blind. After Tim put in his hour as a "blind" person and then went home, a lightbulb turned on in my brain. I told my unsuspecting brothers to blindfold themselves. When they convinced me they couldn't see anything, I directed them to a certain box in my room, filled with my books and magazines. As they opened it, I told them to shuffle through the items inside.

When I saw the magazine I wanted, I shouted, "Wait, that's it! Bring it here." My brothers, still blindfolded, set the buried treasure on my wheelchair tray in front of me. In my most commanding voice, I instructed, "Okay, you know I can't move my arms, so turn the pages." After a moment of their compliance, I shouted, "STOP!" I smiled, looking at the most beautiful model ever featured in the *Sports Illustrated* swimsuit issue. I then told my brothers to put the magazine back in the middle of the box and to put the box back in the closet. I congratulated them on a job well done and never told them what I was looking at. I don't think they ever found out.

Obviously, my injury hadn't decreased my interest in girls! I still liked girls. A lot! I still wanted to date, just like before. I still wanted to get married someday and raise a family. I still hoped those dreams were possible for me. And who knows? Maybe this swimsuit model might want a guy like me.

I'd been at my mom's for about two months when my dad turned the dining room in the house I grew up in into a bedroom for me. This was great because I wanted to live closer to my school and friends. Plus, there were so many wonderful memories for me there. I started to split the week between my mom's and my dad's.

Since my accident, I had not spent as much time with my dad as I had with my mom. He was remarried with a new family and had a job, so he was pretty busy. That's not to say that he hadn't been there for me or hadn't been comforting or helpful. I loved my dad, and I knew that he loved me. But I missed the camaraderie and fun we used to have, and I was slowly seeing that closeness slipping.

Even after I began living at his house a few days a week, we still did not spend much time together. Before my accident, a lot of our interaction involved physical activities, like sports, yard work, and horsin' around. Now that I couldn't physically move, it felt like he was withdrawing. I also began to wonder if he had previously been living vicariously through my athletic successes.

As I was struggling with that new reality, only eight months after my accident, an uplifting and positive opportunity came my way. A family friend handed my dad a flyer about a certain world-famous faith healer coming to a nearby town. My dad was skeptical, but passed it on to me as was requested. *Wow!* It caught me off guard.

My faith in God was strong, and I had no doubt that He could heal anyone whenever He wanted and could use anyone He wanted to perform that healing. It could be through a healer's touch or a scientist's cure. However my healing might happen didn't matter to me, because I felt fairly confident that someday I would be healed. To reinforce my belief, one day while I was doing errands downtown, out of nowhere, a man ran up to me and exclaimed, "Hey, man, never give up! I was in a wheelchair for years, and then one day, I woke up and was healed!" I believed him.

A lot of my positive attitude about being physically healed or restored was innate and maybe from God too, but some also came from a book my dad gave to me. The title was *See You at the Top*, by the world-famous motivational speaker Zig Ziglar. After reading his book, I was so full of positivity that I completely believed that I would walk again. In fact, I had watched a video about a friend of Mr. Ziglar's, titled *The Miracle Man*. The video told the story of a guy who had been paralyzed, but because of his strong, positive attitude, he was walking just eight months after his accident.

I saw no reason I couldn't do the same. I did, however, give myself a few extra months, just to be on the conservative side. I secretly predicted that I could be walking ten months after my accident, which would be just in time for the Senior Ball and graduation. How convenient! I was so hyped on positive thinking that I convinced myself that I might just walk into my Senior Ball and surprise everyone. Can you imagine how awesome that would be? I could picture myself walking, maybe not perfectly, but walking, nonetheless, down "Grand March," and all my friends would be so stunned they wouldn't be able to stop cheering and crying! For months I lived with that vision in my head.

So now, all of a sudden, I wondered if I might be healed through this man, this healer from the flyer...and be healed this coming weekend. *Wow!* My mind was racing, but I knew better than to get "flipped out" excited. Even though I eagerly hoped to be healed, I didn't have to be a rocket scientist to know that there were conmen waiting to prey on the naïve. I had no intention of being fooled or conned.

My intrigue was definitely piqued though. I called my mom to ask what she thought about this so-called faith healer. Her response first stunned me and then solidified my expectations that I would be healed through this man. "David," she said, "you have met this man before. When you were just a baby in Panama, this man performed at a local event. I met him, and he held you in his arms."

Whoa! In my mind—a mind desperately desiring to have a functioning body again and believing that it would happen soon—I thought that maybe I had some special connection with this man. Not in a weird way, but maybe just that our connection so early in my life gave me an extra point in my favor. Now, I was more excited than ever!

All through my week at school, I could hardly keep this exciting news to myself. Without giving anything away, I did, though, ask my best friend, Erik, if he could drive me somewhere on Saturday. He said, "Of course!" That's what best friends do.

Friday came, and I went to bed that night with anxious thoughts, as you can imagine.

Tomorrow I might come home walking. I might get out of the car by myself. I might walk into our house and go upstairs to my old bedroom. Tomorrow I might be able to do all the things I used to do. Wow.

Feeling like a kid on Christmas Eve, I went to sleep with hope beyond words! Maybe tomorrow, this horrible nightmare ends, and I get my life back.

I woke up Saturday morning feeling ready for my "Christmas" miracle! Neville helped me with my morning care, just like every morning. It was the same morning routine in a day that might turn out not so ordinary for me. I asked her to show me the flyer again. You know that feeling how sometimes you want to check the details again and again even though you've already checked them a million times. Well, I checked that flyer one more time and suddenly stopped. "Isn't today March 18th?"

"No. Today's the 19th."

I missed the event. I missed it. This is unbelievable! I was quiet for a moment. *How could I have made that mistake?* I let out a sigh. *How did I do that?* I sighed again.

I was stunned. I was sad. But I was not devastated. It took a moment, but in all honesty, part of me knew that, even if this man truly had God's healing power, it might just not have been my time. Deep down I realized that today must just not be the day that God had planned to heal me. That's faith. And that kind of faith can only come from God. I couldn't come up with that faith on my own. God gave me that faith to trust Him in everything, even when I felt my hope of healing crashing down around the wheels of my chair. I am so grateful that God blessed me with such faith.

All this was going on in my head as Neville continued getting me ready for the day, while I silently accepted that my life in a wheelchair would continue.

My senior year of high school continued as well. I pursued my targeted GPA. I pursued cute girls. In fact, I was about to launch myself into the dating world! I was really ready! I had kept in touch with a few girls I had liked before my accident; one in particular was Lori. In fact, now that I was back on campus and seeing her almost every day, I felt it was time to ask her out. I was thinking of something casual, like going to get frozen yogurt. I wasn't nervous about asking her out, but I also wasn't positive she would say yes, considering that I now had a severe disability.

I asked my dad to dial her phone number for me. He then placed the phone against my ear. I could not hold the phone with my fingers, so I pressed the phone against my head with my hand. I only had the arm strength to hold it for about five minutes. I kicked my dad out of the room. Lori and I chatted briefly, and then I asked, "Would you like to get some frozen yogurt with me?"

"Sure!" she replied enthusiastically.

Phew!

I was thrilled, of course. We made plans for the next day. Lori came to my house, looking as pretty as ever. Neville showed her how to load me in the van and strap down my wheelchair, and the two of us were off on my first date since my accident. The entire afternoon, Lori was so sweet and understanding and did not mind at all helping me get in my van and driving us, helping me eat, and tilting me back as I rested on her shoulder. We had a great time! However, after two more dates, we mutually agreed we wanted to be friends only.

Thanks to Lori, I now had the confidence to ask out other girls. I felt somewhat normal again, going out on several dates with other girls, including Shelley. She had always been the "special" one in my life, and I wanted to not only impress her, but to spoil her as a way of saying "thank you for always being so good to me." So I took her to dinner at the fanciest restaurant around. We had a wonderful dinner with great food and great conversation! I still thought of her as such a beautiful and amazing woman! But, sadly, she would soon be leaving again for an out-of-state college, and we knew we would hardly ever see each other.

I enjoyed dating a lot. Each girl was kind and seemed genuinely happy to be with me. I know I really enjoyed being with them. But after every date, I wondered if these girls were dating me because of who I was before my accident, that they were attracted to the former me and not the present me. I never asked, but I always wondered.

I wonder if this is some sort of insecurity on my part. I wonder if I will always wonder this. I wonder if I will ever find a girl who truly loves me, despite this whole disability thing.

As if my acceptance of living my life paralyzed was not enough, I also felt my friends were drifting away into their own lives. We'd grown up being so adventurous, so silly, and so close, but now I sat on the outside looking in. They hung out with one another without me more often. They went on trips and outings without me. It was hard for me. I felt abandoned and rejected and powerless to do anything about it. Again, I didn't ask them about it. I figured if some-one didn't want to spend time with me, I wouldn't tell them to or force them to. Plus, I didn't want them to feel guilty for not including me in everything they did. I knew they still wanted to do adventurous and fun things.

I also knew they still loved and cared about me. Maybe they just weren't sure how to process my accident and how I now fit in the group. They had always known me as out-going and as a leader, but now I was the opposite. I dealt with my sadness by trying to imagine the situation from their point of view. They were on the threshold of adult-hood and consumed with their own plans for college and careers. Plus, none of us had any real understanding or experience of a close friend suddenly becoming severely disabled.

One of the most difficult episodes was when Scott invited Steve to replace me on a trip we had previously planned to Maui. I wasn't mad at Scott or Steve. I under-stood that the trip would be a challenge for me, and of course, I knew Scott would still want to go to Maui, but this "change of plans that left me out" hit me hard with the reality of how my life was forever different.

I guess it's just another thing I have to deal with.

My last two months of high school were filled with both joy and disappointment. Unfortunately, I was still severely paralyzed with hope dwindling that I would regain any function, much less walk again. I was sensing my friends leaving me behind as they went on with their lives. I was sad, frustrated, and hurt, but I was gradually facing and accepting the reality of these two issues. As hard as it was, I continued on. Maybe the old cliché is true—"Time heals all wounds." Though I must admit, I still believed God could heal me, but His time for that was not as soon as I hoped and prayed for.

One bright spot was the Senior Ball. There was no way I was going to miss that! After three shopping trips to Sacramento (yes, three!), I found the perfect tuxedo to rent. On any regular day, the wide tan chest strap that kept me from falling out of the wheelchair was embarrassingly obvious as it was on the outside of my shirts, but for this fancy night, I asked a family friend to unstitch the sides of my tuxedo jacket and shirt so the strap would be hidden. After all, my date, Cinnamon, was one of the prettiest girls on campus, so "looking good" was a priority!

As it turned out, while I was getting "put together" in the kitchen, she called to say that she was running late, because her dress needed last-minute sewing. It was worth the wait, for when she walked through our front door, she looked stunning! The delay, however, caused us to miss our dinner reservations at an expensive restaurant, so for the fun of it, we went to McDonalds. Believe it or not, some of the other Senior Ball couples were there in their tuxedos and gowns!

By the time we arrived at the Veterans Hall, the dance floor was packed with high school seniors. Parents admired us all from the bleachers as each couple heard their names announced while strolling down the red carpet in the Grand March. When our names came over the loud-speaker, Cinnamon wheeled me down the red carpet while the entire hall erupted in cheers. I was grinning ear-to-ear, and inside I felt elated by their show of support and love. I later remembered that I had hoped to be walking on that special night, but in that moment, I wasn't thinking about that at all!

To put it mildly, my Senior Ball was a blast! Whenever the DJ played a fast song, Cinnamon wheeled me all around the dance floor, zooming in and out between our friends. For the slow songs, we stayed in one spot, and she sat sideways on my lap with her arm around me. The entire evening was fantastic! That was such an amazing and special time; a time I could not have imagined only ten months before lying in the hospital.

Then, within a matter of weeks, it was the end of school and the end of my high school career. Amid my excitement and reflection, I still had two events to attend before graduation day. The first event was the annual Nevada Union Athletic Awards night held in the gymnasium. As the bleachers filled up with families, students, and teachers, I sat with a few dozen other student athletes in the center of the gym. One by one, as each of our names were called, we walked, or in my case rolled, up to the front to receive our awards. When my name was called, my friend Steve wheeled my chair to the podium as my soccer coach, Coach Crowe, took the microphone to introduce me to the crowd. "During the spring of last year," he announced, "David Kline was elected to be our team captain for his senior year. Even though some pretty significant circumstances got in the way, he has made such an impact, not just on our team, but on the entire school, that we are honoring him with his Nevada Union varsity letters." The entire crowd rose to their feet in applause. I felt the same overwhelming joy I had experienced at my Senior Ball. Receiving the NU letters was a true honor that was incredibly sincere and thoughtful!

The second event, the following night, was my school's baccalaureate, a traditional religious ceremony to commemorate graduates. The theater was used for this event, and I was on stage with the other students who chose to be there. To open the service, a local pastor shared a short sermon and a prayer prepared for us graduates. A few students had been chosen to say a few words as part of the ceremony; I was one of them. I was not nervous, maybe because of my speech class and because I had prepared a few remarks. When it was my turn, I was wheeled up to the microphone. With the support of my friends and peers behind me, I looked out onto all the faces in the audience. I saw my mom. I saw my friends' parents. I saw several teachers I'd had. Every eye was on me. You could have heard a pin drop. I took a deep breath and said, "The Lord has been a part of my life for many years and even more so since July 7th of last year. Before my accident, I competed in several sports, including soccer, basketball, and track. Whenever I competed in a track meet, before each race, as I took my mark, I would silently quote Isaiah 40:31, one of my favorite Bible verses. Though I can no longer run, I still quote this verse as it still applies to my life today. It reads, 'But those who wait on the LORD shall renew their strength; they shall mount up with wings like eagles, they shall run and not be weary, they shall walk and not faint.'" As I returned back to my place on stage, I saw tears streaming down many faces in the audience. It was in this moment that God reminded me of how He could use my life and story to inspire others.

And then came graduation morning, eleven months to the day of my accident! In less than a year, I had endured spinal surgery, almost died twice in ICU, spent many nights in the hospital with pneumonia, realized all my expectations as an athlete were dashed, spent four months in rehab learning how to live without moving, returned to my beloved high school to complete my senior year, adjusted to dictating rather than writing my assignments, sang in the Boys' Chorus, served on the student council, danced at my prom, and now I was graduating with my class and with honors.

To be honest, I wasn't patting myself on the back (not that I could do that anymore!). With or without my disability, I expected to earn a 3.5/4.0 GPA. What made me so happy was knowing that I had graduated despite my disability, something that easily could have stalled my education.

My graduation ceremony was poignant, I must admit. Family members arrived from around the state, including Nana and my aunt Cheryl. Also, to accommodate my wheelchair, volunteers had built a ramp on either side of the stage. My friend Steve pushed me up the ramp, and the principal announced our names. The stadium filled with applause, and my graduating class jumped out of their seats cheering. Every graduate since that day has walked or rolled up those ramps to receive a diploma.

Those ramps were short, whereas my journey to them had been long. I thank God that even though my head hit the sand hard, my brain was not injured. That one miracle has made a difference in every part of my life. That's how my mom remembers her first sight of me in the emergency room. When I told her, "Hi, Mom," even though we didn't know the extent of my injuries, she knew, in that moment, she still had *me*. I thank my mom too, for she was obviously a big help in me completing my senior year and graduating.

Senior Ball with Cinnamon.

On my way to my high school graduation!

CHAPTER 9

Now that the frenzy of graduation was behind me, I wanted to enjoy my summer before starting the next stage of my life: college. With high school over and warmer weather outside, one of the things I wanted to do was try and spend more time with my friends.

The parents of my friend Dave owned a property with a huge lake, with a covered deck, diving board, floating dock, rope swing, plus a kitchen area with a barbeque and fire pit. Yes, this was as close to heaven as I could imagine. No, I couldn't swim or dive anymore, but just hanging out there with my friends was still so pleasant! On that beautiful summer day, I loved sitting under the towering pines, enjoying the conversations and joking around with my best buds! As the sun set, we lit a fire in the fire pit and circled around, feeling like we could talk forever; that is, until we stuffed our faces with s'mores followed by our predictable marshmallow fights soon after! When the evening chill approached, I was wheeled up closer to the fire. Ah, perfect. It all felt like I was back living a "normal" life.

Almost.

It would only be another couple of hours later, as Neville was getting me ready for bed, that "normal" shifted to the reality of my "new normal" when she suddenly said, "Oh no! You've got burn blisters on your knees."

I'm no Einstein, but it wasn't hard to know where those came from!

Wow, there's always something! Even the littlest thing can cause a problem. Mental note: Remember, I don't have feeling in my legs. Always be aware of heat sources and my proximity to them.

When July 7th rolled around, I "celebrated" my accident's first anniversary with a visit to the UCD Med Center. Many of the nurses greeted me and my mom with smiles and shock at how well I looked! When I shared about my days at Shriners and that I'd just graduated with honors with my class, they beamed! I assured them that without their loving care in those earliest days, I might not have accomplished so much. After we said our good-byes, my mom and I traveled down into the bowels of the hospital to the physical therapy room. I was so happy to see Ron Silver, the very kind physical therapist who had worked with me before I had transferred to Shriners. His face lit up when he saw me! It only took a few minutes of catching up before he asked me, "Are you able to feed yourself?"

Feeling like I was disappointing him, I had to tell him, "No. I have the hand brace with the slit in it, but I just don't have the dexterity and ability to stab or scoop my food."

Ron rushed to his desk, opened a drawer, and rushed back with some contraption that can only be described as a "right-angle pocket," which he slid into the slit in my hand brace. Next thing I knew, he'd inserted a fork into that right-angle pocket, so instead of my fork pointing straight out, it now pointed down. I simulated the motion of stabbing and scooping food. Wah-lah!

"I can do it!" I said with a smile of sudden independence!

That's all it took! One man to say, "Try this," and from that moment forward, I could now feed myself without relying on someone else. Not only did this "small" practical suggestion give me greater independence, but for the sake of my self-esteem, I could now look less dependent. As much as I enjoyed cute girls helping me eat, I would enjoy even more eating meals with cute girls while feeding myself.

Wow, what an unexpected gift!

As my mom and I turned to leave, I was still saying, "Thank you so much, Ron!" I love unexpected joys!

As fall approached and college loomed, I worried about how well I'd do maneuvering around a huge campus, finding classmates willing to take notes for me, and how my stamina would hold up with a full schedule. To ease all those worries, I enrolled for two night classes through a local community college.

Because of my interest in houses and architecture, I took a real estate class, which ended up with me thinking seriously about pursuing a law degree in that field. My other class was speech, chosen by me specifically because it was taught by my favorite teacher from high school, Mr. Brown. His college speech class was just as great, if not better, than his high school speech class! His humor and out-of-the-box assignments kept us interested as we laughed our way through the semester! Oh, and yes, speaking in front of such a friendly, fun-loving class rebuilt my confidence that I could speak in front of others! Thank you, Mr. Brown!

While all this frivolity of my fall semester was happening, another "reality" moment could not be far behind. Neville, my ever faithful-from-the-beginning caregiver, the one who had helped me transition smoothly from hospital life to home life, my friend, needed to move on. Sure, I understood situations arise that cause shifts in people's lives, but Neville was my "angel." It was a sad good-bye. Before she left, she helped me find my second attendant of my "disabled career." Lisa was a young nursing student, the mother of two young children, and, like Neville, was also very caring. Neville and I spent a few days training her in my routine and my preferences for my care.

About this time, I moved from my mom's house back to my childhood home with my dad and his new family to be closer to my friends and my school. My mom though was designing plans for a basement addition to her house that would be completely wheelchair accessible. She wanted me to have my own space. When I shared that I wanted to be back in town, she still kept on with the addition. She was determined to give me an accessible place whenever I was with her. She set up donation jars in local grocery stores and publicized that funds would be needed to help with the excessive costs of building this accessible apartment, including a staircase wheelchair lift. I appreciated her effort, but my mind was made up.

Besides, a wheelchair lift would just be an unnecessary expense; I might be walking again soon.

My dad also converted his garage into an apartment built for me. Obviously, being on ground level, there was no accessibility issue there. Having my own place in my old home and near my friends was a boost for my independence and freedom. From time to time, I'd stay at my mom's house in the main floor bedroom, for I enjoyed spending time with her.

On one of my visits at her house one afternoon, I had a very dark thought. A few people have asked me if I ever considered suicide after my accident. This was the one moment that I did. I didn't actually *consider* it, but the thought crossed my mind. The new stairs in her living room leading down to "my" new apartment were very steep.

One day, when I wasn't feeling my normal chipper self, as I was sitting at the top of those stairs looking down, I thought, *I could push my chair just enough to take me right down those stairs and end it all.* I paused for a moment. *I'd probably just end up breaking my neck.* That thought made me laugh, and that was the extent of my "suicidal" thoughts.

After only a few months living at my dad's, he came in to my room to have a talk. His business was having financial problems, causing him some hardship. This was not news to me, as I had heard him discuss this before. But then he dropped the bomb. "I'm afraid you can't live here anymore; you're just too much of a burden." Stunned, I sat there in silence.

I didn't understand. My caregivers and medical supplies were paid for by the state and by insurance. I sometimes got free government food from the local center. I didn't see how I was a financial burden. There was nothing I could say. My nonconfrontational manner kicked in, and

I remained silent, comforted by the knowledge that my mom would welcome me back. I immediately called her.

She said, "David, you know how broke I am right now. I can't even pay my bills. I'm sorry."

Wow, my own parents won't let me stay with them? They've been so supportive! My mom's been with me every step of the way since my accident. Why not now? Don't parents go all out and do whatever they have to do to help their child in need!

This was hard for me to fathom. After a time and the shock of this started to soften, I began to evaluate the "why" of it all. This was so atypical of them that I figured I was being used as a pawn by both parents to get back at the other. I learned later the extent of how broke both my parents were and the stress and hardship that that caused. Whatever the reason though, I had never felt lonelier in my life.

Neither one of my parents would budge, so I was forced to find another home. The problem was that I had nowhere to go, except to find a motel until I could figure out what to do. As Lisa packed me and all my belongings into my van which was parked in the driveway of the house where I had grown up, I tried to accept that I'd been asked to leave my own home.

We found the cheapest motel in town, but just before I checked in, I got the idea to call my friend's mom to ask if I could stay at her house. Erik was away at college. I knew his room was unoccupied at that time, and I knew too that his mom, Carol, would do anything she could for me. I was not surprised, just so grateful, when she said, "David, get over here right now!"

What a relief! I hardly had any money and certainly didn't want to be a burden to her, so I planned to only stay a week and live off the food that I brought—apples and granola. Even with her generosity, it was an excruciatingly emotional week for me.

During that week, Lisa and I decided a move to Rocklin, forty-five minutes away, would be good for both of us. We could rent a house, and I'd enroll for my second semester at Sierra College. Within a few days, we were moving into an affordable two-bedroom house.

I told my mom and dad, and they both supported my decision. Believe it or not, though I still felt hurt, my parents and I still talked often on the phone, and moving away didn't mean I didn't see them. In fact, my mom transferred her schooling to Sierra College for a semester and even helped wheel me to my first class. Neither my parents nor I ever discussed or even mentioned the event from just a couple weeks prior. I acted like nothing had happened, even though my heart was still breaking. *I am so nonconfrontational.*

I was doing my best to move on with the plans I was making for my life. I was in college now and was living on my own. I had Lisa, who was a helpful and caring attendant, but unfortunately, her kids moving in with us added a challenge I hadn't planned on. A month later, her new boyfriend moved in too. I not only had the nonstop noise of her rambunctious sons, but now there were other noises in the night. Let's just say I didn't get a lot of sleep those days.

Despite all those distractions, I focused on my classes and staying healthy. I really enjoyed my college classes and being part of the student body. My professors and classmates helped me every way they could. To my pleasant surprise, my college classes were manageable, even easy. My worry about having the stamina turned out to not be an issue either. I should've taken more classes! And wow, there were so many attractive girls on campus! One of them partnered with me for a group project. Nice!

And because of my diligent practice, stretching, and strengthening exercises, my arms were getting stronger and my dexterity, handwriting, and typing were improving. I could hardly believe I was able to type my own homework assignments. I love seeing improvement!

After a year of only four junior college classes that all turned out to be fairly easy, it was time for me to take a bigger step in my education. I just didn't know what size step I was ready to make or wanted to make. My aunt Cheryl (my mom's sister) in southern California kept hyping up California State University, Northridge (CSUN), which was located just a few minutes from her house. I hadn't even heard of that school before. "They have the best adaptive physical therapy program in the country," she kept reminding me. That sounded good, but moving away to southern California was too big of a step. I knew though at some point I would need to transfer to a four-year university, but when and where?

As my indecision and procrastination continued on into the summer, my aunt Cheryl knew that I needed a push out the door. Without my knowledge, she went ahead and enrolled me at CSUN for that fall. I wasn't mad; I knew I didn't have to go. I was mostly a little nervous. Deep down I knew I should go, and since I didn't have a better plan, I glumly said, "Okay, I'll go." That was not my finest moment of showing gratitude.

I began to make plans for my life-changing journey toward earning my college degree. I also began to seriously contemplate my future and the importance of having a direction for my life. *This decision could affect the rest of my life. It is time to pull up my boot straps and take my life seriously. This is my life. As of today, and most likely for quite a while, I am in a wheelchair. What am I going to do with my life? What am I going to do to not let this thing beat me?*

One facet of growing up and moving forward in my life concerned my independence—or lack thereof. If I wanted greater independence, I would need to shift from a manual to a motorized wheelchair, which would mean I could control and go where I wanted without requiring someone to push me. With the start of school only one month away, I knew I needed practice controlling a more "technological" chair. (On a side note, I prefer the term *motorized chair* because *electric chair* just sounds kind of horrific.)

Since it had been over a year since I had used this chair, I called my friend Kathleen to invite her to go on a walk with me so that I could practice. We chose to take our walk on Independence Trail, a smooth dirt trail that wound through the woods above the Yuba River for a couple of miles. For those of us longing to enjoy nature but limited in mobility, Independence Trail was specifically designed to accommodate us wheelchair users. *I love that!*

The next morning, Lisa helped me with my normal routine and then picked me up out of bed and into my motorized chair. I touched the joystick controller with my hand and instantly recalled how touchy and sensitive it could be. Like my experience at Shriners Hospital, I quickly figured out how to control the chair fairly well.

Kathleen came over, and we headed out to the trail. It was a beautiful, warm summer day. The trail was fairly smooth with just a few small bumps, and my ability to drive the chair accurately was not a problem. We talked and laughed and enjoyed our time together. It took about twenty-five minutes to reach our destination, a series of wooden, switchback wheelchair ramps that led down to a deck along a creek. We paused there for a few moments while Kathleen took off her shoes and waded into the refreshing, cool creek. I was resting too. My right arm, the arm I used to control the joystick, was exhausted! I was not accustomed to using and holding up my arm for a continuous twenty-five minutes.

On our way back to the entrance of the trail and to my van, I finally had to stop after about five minutes; my arm was too tired. Kathleen was her usual kind, caring, and accommodating self and offered to push me back the rest of the way. I accepted. She was so understanding that I wasn't really embarrassed by my weakness; I was mostly just grateful for her help. I instructed her on how to unlock the wheels and disengage the motor, and we were off.

Pushing a heavy motorized wheelchair was not an easy task, especially on a dirt trail! The front wheels seemed to have a mind of their own. Kathleen found this out the hard way. There was a section of the trail where the path leaned slightly down to the left where winter rainwater must have carved its own path. My front wheels felt the angled tilt of the trail floor and abruptly turned my chair to the left and, in an instant, tilted me and my chair over to the left. Thankfully, there was a hillside cliff wall to the left of the trail that broke my fall. My head and shoulders and chair were all leaning against this wall of dirt. I was fine; nothing was injured. But Kathleen was so worried!

"Are you okay?" she shouted out.

"I'm fine," I replied.

"I'm so sorry, David," she said, feeling like it was her fault.

"Don't apologize," I comforted. "It was totally an accident; it's just the way the chair rolls.

She tried to pull my chair back over onto all four wheels, but it was far too heavy (over 300 pounds with the combined weight of the chair and me). Her second attempt to right me was pretty clever. She wriggled her petite frame between the dirt wall and my chair, with her back against the dirt wall. Then she lifted her knees, put her feet against my chair, and pushed with her legs. My chair leaned and leaned until finally it fell flat onto all four wheels. Phew! Now we both were exhausted!

"Good job!" I told her.

"Thanks," she said tiredly. "Has this ever happened to you before?" she asked.

"Honestly, no." I smiled.

Kathleen smiled back, and we continued very carefully back to my van.

CHAPTER 10

S ummer was ending, and once again, my attendant Lisa packed up my belongings and me in my van. This time though, we drove six hours south to Northridge, California. I was moving into brand-new dorms at CSUN. Each dorm unit had two bedrooms, one bathroom, a living room, a dining room, a kitchen, and a patio and would house four students. The school generously accommodated my disability needs by giving me my own dorm unit, with the second bedroom available for my caregiver. With two kids, a boyfriend, and a life back home, Lisa only stayed until I could hire a new attendant. His name was JC, and he was a nice young man from Venezuela. *JC* was short for *Julius Caesar*. Seriously.

My aunt Cheryl was thrilled, of course, that I chose CSUN. Right away, she took me shopping to furnish my dorm. *She is so thoughtful and generous!* Once I had furniture, it was time for my introductory journey into the CSUN campus. With thirty-five thousand students, it was huge!

I was both excited and a little nervous. Finally, we found the registration office, and I signed all the required forms, made it official, and received my class schedule for a full load of fifteen units. I continued to take general education classes like I had done during my first year of college at Sierra College. Cheryl and I then toured the campus that would now be my life for the next few years.

My first priority was to locate the Center of Achievement, where I would enjoy the benefits of a cutting-edge master's program in Adaptive PE. I had researched this Adaptive PE class before enrolling at CSUN, and it was one of the main reasons I chose to attend this school.

We were warmly welcomed by Dr. Britten, the director, and his right-hand gal, Jenny. Jenny, a cute, friendly girl, coincidentally just about my age. They showed us the main activity room filled with exercise equipment and tables for stretching. From what I saw, it was obvious that Dr. Britten had developed a world-class program!

The final stop of our campus tour was the Disabled Students Services department. The nice people there would be assisting me with my classroom needs, including note taking and test proctoring.

On my first day of school, I left my dorm building along with a long trail of other students walking their way to the campus. Within minutes, I was caught up in the energy of it all! The campus itself was alive with activity. There were students everywhere! And oh yes—so many cute girls! And even though I'd grown up in a very small, some would say "quaint" hometown, I didn't feel overwhelmed. I felt ready. I did have to be a little brave though. Because my handwriting was extremely slow and not the neatest, I had to speak up and ask the class if anyone would let me make photocopies of their notes. Thankfully, there were always students who offered to help.

Before long, I was definitely in the groove of college life. My classes were going well, and my professors were interesting and informative, but there was something that was making me very sad. I called my mom. "Mom, I'm lonely. I haven't made any new friends, and I don't think I will. And what's really weird for me is that no one here knows anything about my background. Unlike high school, no one here knows that I was an athlete, that I was outgoing, that I was popular. At school now, all they see is a guy in a wheelchair."

My mom listened patiently, holding back her tears.

I continued, "The guys in my classes and in my dorm don't know that just two years ago I could have beaten them in any track and field event. I could have outplayed them on any soccer field. And the girls don't know that just two years ago I had a very fit and athletic body and was outgoing and fun. It's weird. And frustrating. And lonely, Mom."

Being my mom, she tried her best to comfort and encourage. I'm sure it was hard for her to hear her son express such sadness. She promised me that my personality would soon shine and everyone would notice! Sure enough, the day came when I finally got the chance to give my fellow students a glimpse of not only my personality, but also my intelligence. And ironically, it happened in my psychology class.

The professor had chosen his favorite student papers to read to the class. To my surprise, he read mine! Not only was my paper well written, it was also a very intense story with a totally unexpected ending! I don't think my classmates anticipated how clever my story was, especially coming from someone so quiet. From their smiles and their applause, I definitely sensed a shift. At least now students looked in my direction.

My favorite class of the year was my daily Adaptive PE class. I enjoyed working out. The "gym" had a full range of cutting-edge exercise equipment, including the tilt table I had used at Shriners Hospital. They also had an Uppertone weight machine for quadriplegics to tone and strengthen their upper body, plus an arm cycler for cardiovascular exercise. It felt good physically and mentally to work my muscles hard again. I also enjoyed the staff. Jenny, Becky, Marty, and Dr. Sam were so kind, so fun, and so helpful. They became like my family away from home.

I also wanted to find a church family I could fellowship with while I was in southern California. My relationship with Jesus was still the core of who I was. I opened up the phone book, found a Calvary Chapel near the campus, and gave them a call. "I'm new to the area, have been going to Calvary Chapels most of my life, and am wondering if you have a Bible study group for college students." I learned that Chris and Jim led a study each week. We made arrangements to have these two guys pick me up for the next study.

Jim and Chris were graphic design majors at CSUN and had been friends for a long time. They were more than willing to come get me and to learn how to strap my wheelchair down in the van. We drove to their friend Robert's apartment for the Bible study. There were probably a dozen college students there, including a couple cute girls, who I learned were the girlfriends of Jim and Chris. *Oh well.*

After I met everyone and we had chatted for a bit, we started worship with a couple on guitars leading the singing. Then Chris taught us a study from the Bible. I was impressed. It was not a superficial feeling, but a genuine feeling in all of these people. I began to quickly perceive, week after week, that these people truly loved God. They didn't just talk the talk, they walked the walk. I found that impressive—and admirable. It was something I wanted in my own life. I had grown up with Christian friends, but these guys here really lived their faith in all aspects of their lives.

One small example occurred at a birthday party for one of the girls. Halfway through the party, someone took out a guitar, and then we spent the next two hours singing and praising God. I had never seen that happen at a birthday party before. This was a time of real spiritual growth for me. I truly welcomed it.

Something else I welcomed was a surprise visit from my mom, Jon, and Adam for my twentieth birthday. It was so good to see them! I gave them a tour of the campus, and we went to my favorite restaurant for dinner, The Cheesecake Factory. This would be the first of a number of surprise visits from them.

In the spring of that year, I had a physical setback. There was an extra part on the back of my wheelchair that I didn't need, so my caregiver, JC, tucked it out of the way. Unfortunately, he tucked it in a bad location. We didn't realize until it was too late that that part ended up putting pressure on my back where I have no feeling. A small pressure sore had developed, and once again, the only way for those things to heal was for them to have no pressure. Hearing the news from JC was frustrating and disheartening. Right off the bat, we knew I'd have to stay in bed for at least a week. *I already know how these things can go. I wonder if this will take as long to heal as it did last time.* As a precaution, I let my friends, note takers, and professors know I'd be out for awhile.

That turned out to be a wise move because, just like my senior year of high school, my pressure sore kept me in bed for a month. I thought I had learned patience by this time in my life, but this experience increased it even more! After this event, I began insisting that my skin be checked every day. From then on, each morning, if my skin showed any sign of irritation or pressure, I would not get out of bed that day. It wasn't worth the risk.

I don't want to be stuck in bed for a month ever again.

With the assistance of friends, JC, and my aunt Cheryl, I continued to complete my schoolwork from bed during that month. Despite the challenges and after a lot of hard work, I earned all As and Bs that year.

With my first year at CSUN completed, I headed back to Grass Valley for summer vacation. I missed my family, friends, and hometown. I'd already arranged an apartment for the summer, and JC agreed to travel with me. If he had not been able to go with me, I probably would have stayed in Northridge. Although my care is not difficult, it's much easier if the attendant has been trained.

Over the nine months that JC had been my attendant, he and I had become good friends. We joked around a lot, which I didn't do as much with Neville or Lisa. When my friends would come over to visit, JC would hang out with us.

As easygoing as JC was, I did learn that summer about a fault that he had. In the rare event that JC drank alcohol, he would drink way too much. One warm summer evening, JC asked if he could borrow my van and go into town. I was at the apartment alone, which was fine. I was often alone since I did not require an attendant at all times. In fact, because my attendants lived with me, I usually did enjoy those rare moments I had by myself.

After he'd been gone a few hours, the time I usually started to get ready for bed came and went. Without his help, I couldn't go to the bathroom or get into bed; 10 p.m. turned into 11 p.m. I was beginning to get worried about my care, plus worried about him *and* my van. When midnight arrived, I called my mom in Folsom. She woke up Jon and Adam, and they all headed up my way. I also left a message for my friend Scott, asking for his help. Then I called the police. They had been waiting for my call.

They had JC in custody for drunk driving. Apparently, he had gone to a bar. After drinking excessively, he got in my van, thinking he could drive home. Bad idea. Within minutes, the police pulled him over. Obviously not thinking straight, he tried to hide behind the driver's seat. When the officer slid open the sliding door of my van, JC, scared, tried to grab the officer's gun. Fortunately, the officer quickly determined that JC was drunk out of his mind and was not intending to harm him. JC was handcuffed and driven to the police station.

When the police began questioning him, the first question was, "What is your name?" Of course, JC, being an honest man even in his drunken state, answered, "I'm Julius Caesar." I can just picture him in his drunken Venezuelan accent repeating, "I'm Julius Caesar! I'm Julius Caesar!" I'm sure the officers thought it was as hilarious as I did, but they still had a job to do, so JC spent the night under their care. In the meantime, I really needed to pee!

Scott was the first to arrive to help me out. He, like my mom and dad, had been taught how to help me with a catheter. After that problem was taken care of, he picked me up out of my chair and put me in bed. *What a relief!* At that point, my mom and brothers arrived. With all of them there, I told them the "Julius Caesar" story. They all cracked up and thought it was one of the funniest things they had ever heard.

JC was released the next morning. I'd never seen him so embarrassed, and I'm pretty sure he thought I would fire him. If I did, then there'd be no one there to help me with my care. Plus, he was a friend, a friend who had made a mistake. I forgave him, and we never had an episode like that again.

The summer was harder than I had expected, not because of drunk caregivers, but because of all that I physically couldn't do. For most of my life, my summers were filled with swimming at the river or lake, playing soccer and other sports, jogging, exploring the woods, playing, and the list goes on. I loved the sun and warmth of summer, but my reality now confronted me with all I was missing.

I sat in my wheelchair in the apartment, knowing my friends were having a blast doing all those things I used to do. I even was jealous of little things, like how easy it was for others to just hop in a car and go to the store. Some days, all this hit me pretty hard. Some days, I just wanted to cry. But in front of others, I didn't pout, I didn't mope, I didn't complain. It wouldn't have helped or changed anything. I would just get quiet for a day and mentally deal with my reality.

Through it all, I would try to remind myself that God must be doing something and that He must have a plan and a reason. I had to believe that was true! It wasn't easy though. Most of the time I tried not to dwell on the things I couldn't do; I didn't want a pity party. If I stayed busy, this sadness rarely appeared.

It didn't help my mood that I ended up having to spend much of that summer resting in bed because my bottom was getting tired of me sitting on it—again. *Ugh.*

It was at these times that I created a kind of poetic prayer. It was like my way of asking God to heal me. Each night before I went to sleep, this is what I would pray: "Please grant me a deep sleep, just shy of the deepest. May visions of strength and motion make merry mine eyes. May my present reality be like a fleeting vapor, and may You restore me before I die." In the morning, I would wake up and realize that my prayer had not been answered. *Oh well.*

I knew that some people had given up on God when their prayers had not been answered, but I just tried to focus on the fact that God saw the big picture. Maybe He needed me in this physical state for a reason. Maybe He wanted to use me to help someone. I've heard it said before that God *always* answers prayers. It's either "Yes," "No," or "Wait." I knew each morning that the answer that moment was not yes. I didn't know if the answer was no, so I just went with that He wanted me to wait. I just trusted Him and kept keepin' on. *We'll see what tomorrow brings.*

Falling asleep after my bedtime prayers, I often had very interesting dreams. Sometimes I could still walk. I could run. Other times I was in my wheelchair. Once I dreamt I was in my wheelchair in the kitchen. I needed something from an upper cabinet, so I stood up, grabbed it, and sat back down. I had another dream where I was running with a friend. I yelled to him, "Slow down! You know I'm paralyzed!" My soccer dreams were both wonderful and tragic, because even though I could run, I never got to play. Something always prevented me from getting into the game. I might be sitting on the sidelines eager to play, but my cleats were locked in the trunk or I didn't have my uniform or my coach wouldn't put me in. It was agonizing! Still, I did love dreaming though. In my dreams was the only time I got to move. I got to feel.

Jenny and I in the Center of Achievement.

Marty (right) in front of some of the exercise equipment at the Center.

My childhood friend Kim, JC, and I hanging out in my dorm

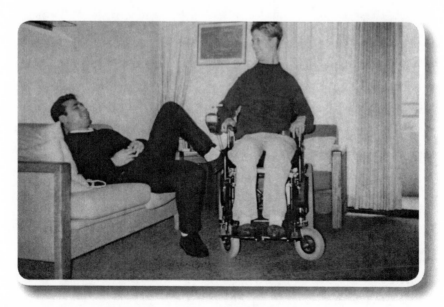

Chris makes himself feel comfortable in my living room.

CHAPTER 11

At summer's end, JC and I headed back down to Los Angeles for my sophomore year. I continued general education classes and Adaptive PE, plus I took the Adaptive Sports class. Adaptive Sports was pretty much the way it sounds—sports were adapted in a way that people with disabilities could participate. I played sports like badminton and tennis with a racquet taped to my arm. My able-bodied assistants cheered every time I hit the ball or birdie. To be honest, after all my athletic success before my accident, being congratulated for barely hitting a birdie from a wheelchair felt frustratingly insignificant and pathetic.

The most humiliating moment for me in that class occurred when the assistants brought out the "earth ball." An earth ball is a giant ball, bigger and a bit heavier than a beach ball. Those of us in wheelchairs were divided into two teams, with each team on opposite sides of the volleyball court. Each team had a few able-bodied players to assist. The object was to hit the earth ball over the net to the opposing team. It was hard enough for the able-bodied students to hit the giant ball over the net. How in the world would I be able to hit it over the net? And can you imagine how difficult it would be to also have to maneuver a wheelchair at the same time? That giant ball was just bonkin' us wheelchair players in the head, and there was nothing we could do about it. Bystanders observing this "torture" must have been either humored or horrified. *Who came up with this humiliating idea?!*

Well, looking on the bright side, at least my general education classes were going well. I was enjoying them and was earning very good grades. As my junior year loomed on the horizon, it was time for me to declare my major, which would impact not only my options for a career, but also, potentially, the quality of my health for the rest of my life. I needed a major that could land me a job that provided both a good income and health benefits. Even with a severe disability, there were still many good career options open for me. My mom always thought I would make a good psychologist.

So I added psychology to the list, but it was my interests in law and real estate that had me seriously considering law school. I could see myself as a real estate developer or real estate lawyer. As I knew a few lawyers from church and from my parents' acquaintances, I sought their input. I learned that none of them enjoyed practicing law. Despite that, I kept law school on my list. And the more and more I thought about it, real estate law appealed to me.

With a potential career goal now in sight, I decided to seek a degree that would give me flexibility in my career choices: speech communication. I highly recommend it. I chose it, first of all, because I enjoyed my speech classes in high school and at Sierra College. The other reason was because I had heard that law schools were getting tired of so many business majors entering their schools and also because they liked students who knew how to speak well. So I made it official and filed the required paperwork to enroll as a speech communication major at California State University, Northridge.

In my time so far at CSUN, my favorite class was English. It's not so much that I loved the subject, but I really enjoyed my professor. She had an easygoing and fun personality and really interacted with us students well.

And then one day, it hit me—I would be of much better use as a teacher than as a lawyer. I had seen so many high school kids head down the wrong path. I truly believed that if I became a high school teacher, my students could have at least one positive influence or receive motivation or encouragement from my attitude and success as a physically challenged person and then maybe they would stay focused or get focused and strive for a healthy, successful life. This lightbulb moment for me seemed very possible and extremely important.

Another reason (and less important reason) I decided to become a teacher is because I thought I would have fun working with high schoolers. I loved my time in high school. I loved to make people laugh, and high schoolers seemed to appreciate my humor (or my attempts at humor).

Those two reasons were all it took for me to switch career paths. It was that simple for me. Plus, I didn't have to change my major for this decision. Speech is not only a great degree for lawyers, journalists, or broadcasters, it is also great for teachers. Speech is how teachers hold their students' attention and intrigue their curiosity. There were many subjects I was good at and could teach, but I decided that my goal was to become a high school speech teacher, just like my favorite teacher, Mr. Brown.

My decision triggered an emotional and spiritual response deep inside me. For these last few years, people had encouraged me that God had a wonderful plan for me and that my accident happened for a reason. I believed this too, and the moment I made the decision to teach, I felt God's assurance that this was His purpose for me. I believed that me becoming a high school teacher was purposed and planned. I even believed it was one of the reasons I had my accident.

That felt good to realize and to acknowledge. It felt good to know that I was following God's plan for me. It felt good to have a purpose. It felt good to have a plan and a goal.

I realized too that my goal was admirable, especially for a person with a disability as serious as mine. I was aware of the fact that most quadriplegics have continual health problems and do not work, due to health and other limiting factors. I though wasn't focused on those limitations. I had set a goal for myself. I was going to achieve it. I didn't see why I couldn't.

Well, it turned out I couldn't go through the year without some health issues. The human body has the potential to do some weird things sometimes. Multiply that a hundredfold for the quadriplegic body!

And so it was that I developed some seriously strange sweats every morning, always about thirty minutes after I got in my wheelchair. The sweats lasted a few hours. The really odd part was that these sweats occurred only on my face. The really, really odd part was that these sweats occurred only on the left side of my face. There was a line down the middle of my face where the left side was wet and the right side was dry. These sweats were so excessive and so consistent that I carried a hand towel with me everywhere I went so that I could wipe the sweat off my face (well, half my face).

It was very embarrassing. Going to school like that, interacting with people, sweating oddly and having to constantly wipe my face, made me a little uncomfortable and frustrated. I talked to doctors about my sweating, but the doctors were no help. It became apparent that, for my own sanity, I needed to accept these symptoms as my body's "new normal." I knew I just had to come to grips with this. I eventually decided not to be so embarrassed by this sweating and constant wiping. It was something that I was going through, and it was reality, for the moment, for me. And thankfully that reality only lasted a few months. I found a homeopathic doctor who treated me with a homeopathic remedy that stopped my weird sweating.

Being physically different, plus that freakish sweating thing, generated feelings of embarrassment, an emotion I had previously not experienced much of. Unfortunately, I was faced with yet another embarrassing issue. My lack of mobility and muscle control translate into a lot of restrictions in simple actions that most people take for granted every day.

For instance, when most people are thirsty, they grab a glass or bottle. Since I could not use my fingers, I had to use both hands together to squish my water bottle so that I could bring it up to my mouth. Way awkward! That's how little kids would do it. For quite some time, due to my embarrassment, I only picked up my bottle when no one was around. I would go thirsty sometimes. It took quite a while for me to get over this. I finally got to the point where I thought, *I want a drink of water. If someone thinks I look awkward, that's his problem.*

I was always confronted with the costs of my caregivers, medical supplies, specialized equipment, and medical care, and financing it all was a serious issue for me. The insurance company that covered all my initial hospital bills and later attendant costs had dropped my dad's policy about a year ago. At that time, I started receiving Supplemental Security Income from the federal government for living expenses. I also qualified for In-Home Supportive Services from the county for attendant costs. I was grateful for that money from taxpayers, but it just wasn't enough to cover everything. I could only pay my caregivers twenty-five dollars a day plus room and board. To help me pay for food and living expenses, my aunt Cheryl started giving me two hundred dollars every month. She was a blessing!

Obviously, I didn't spend much money on entertainment or eating out, because I didn't have any! Like any college kid, I liked to go out, but I rarely did because I had to save every dollar.

Things got worse, though. When the Social Security office asked about additional sources of income, I told them honestly that my aunt was helping me pay for food by giving me two hundred dollars a month. Their response was to lower the amount they gave me by two hundred dollars. Yes, that was a tough one! I felt like I'd just been knocked down again.

Then I remembered to be grateful to be getting something. I was grateful too that my aunt continued to give me two hundred dollars a month. My heart was softened when I thought of all the people with disabilities without any financial options. Still, it was a tough time for me. To make ends meet, I ate nothing but granola and seventy-nine cent frozen dinners.

I will get through this!

Sadly, my dating life was as empty as my bank account. In fact, if my current dating life was measured on the Richter scale, it wouldn't have even registered a tremor. There was no one back home I wanted to date. Shelly had joined the Navy and was somewhere on the opposite side of the planet. I had gone out on many dates before my accident and even a few after in Grass Valley, but I had not asked a girl out since I had been at CSUN.

A challenge I faced was the necessity of changing how I viewed my dating situation. One of my problems was how my brain had been "trained." Before my accident, I asked out any girl I wanted, because I had learned that most of them would say yes. But now, with me having such a serious disability, girls were not as interested in me as before.

I understood physical attraction, and I understood that girls' perception of me would not be the same as I had been accustomed. But my brain was having trouble catching up with this new reality; I still assumed that girls would be interested in me. In the back of my mind though, I knew my dating life would never be that easy again. This was a tough blow.

I tried to keep a sense of humor about it, as I did with most things. For example, I would joke with my friends that I had come up with a technique to meet girls. I told my friends I would sit in front of a vending machine. When a cute girl approached, I would ask for her help. I would look down at my lap and say, "I dropped my quarter. Will you help me get it, please?" Of course, I never actually did that! However, on second thought, maybe I should've tried it.

On a campus of more than thirty thousand students, there were plenty of attractive girls. One in particular crossed my path almost every day on the ten-minute walk between the dorms and the campus. She was a petite girl with dark hair and a very cute face.

I strategized my plan of action. First, I needed to make eye contact. When our paths crossed the next day, I gave her "the look." Just like the old days, her gaze met mine. *Yes! Mission accomplished.* Next, I needed to get a smile from her. On the following day, I gave her the look again, adding a flash of my pearly whites. She gave me a great smile in return. *Excellent.* Now it was time to say hi. When I saw her the next day, I gave her the look and the smile and then said, "Hi." She returned all three. *This is good, very good.* Our little flirtation went on for two weeks.

I knew I needed to step up and introduce myself and talk to her because I really wanted to ask her out. This posed two challenges in my mind. First of all, I wasn't sure she would say yes. Second of all, she would be the first girl I asked out who didn't know me before my accident. She would only know me as a guy with a disability, asking a girl out. This was new territory for me.

The next time I was on my way to school, I spotted her in the distance. *This is it. I'm doin' it.* When were we close enough, we each smiled and said, "Hi." I then paused to introduce myself. She paused in the same instant, making the moment seem entirely mutual. "My name's David," I said, and I reached my arm forward for her to shake my hand.

"I'm Christy," she replied as she shook my hand.

We chatted briefly, and then I asked, "Would you like to go out with me?"

She smiled and said, "Yes."

Success!

She wrote down her phone number for me, and we said good-bye. I could not wipe the smile off my face as I went to class.

We talked on the phone that night and made plans for dinner. When our date night arrived, she walked over to my dorm. She wore a floral dress that just made her look even cuter. I introduced her to JC, who then taught her how to get me in and out of my van. Christy and I went to Benihanas, a popular Japanese restaurant. The food was delicious. The chefs and the atmosphere of the restaurant were fun and entertaining. She laughed at all my jokes. I had a great time. But throughout the night, I realized she was not a girl I wanted a serious relationship with. She was cute and sweet and kind, but not a Christian, and that was a deal breaker for me.

My mom, brothers, Nana, a teddy bear, and my perm.

CHAPTER 12

As my school year was winding down, JC informed me that he was going to be leaving. During our visit to Grass Valley over Christmas vacation, he had fallen in love with a girl from my hometown (yes, I was a little frustrated that he could find a girl in my hometown, but I couldn't). They had been communicating with each other over these last few months and decided that they would get married and move. I was happy for him, but bummed for me; he had been an excellent attendant and a good friend.

His replacement was a man named Chris. He moved in the day JC moved out. Chris was a big guy with a pleasant demeanor. He was really into music, even mixing his own. A lot of our initial conversations revolved around our mutual love of music.

Then came the night, weeks later, as he was getting me ready for bed, he said out of the blue, "Ya know, if you had enough faith, you'd be healed by now." *Wow!* I was already aware of the philosophy that one can do anything with faith, but this philosophy and what Chris said was not scriptural. Faith is huge, but it does not trump God's will. I knew God could heal me if and when He thought was best. And I was not short in the faith department! I kept my cool, I shared what I knew about the subject in the Bible, and we had a good discussion about the issue. We were amiable, even though I could easily have been very offended, for that was quite a thing to say to a person who is a quadriplegic and a Christian.

A short time later, I found out that, while I was attending class, Chris was smoking pot and drinking in the dorms. Apparently, it had become a daily habit for him. Given my physical vulnerability, I had to have a responsible and sober caregiver, which meant I, the dependent quadriplegic, had to fire my caregiver.

I had to muster up the courage. I don't know why, but ever since I was a child, I've avoided confrontations like the plague! Now I needed to be a big boy and say what needed to be said. I had never fired anyone, especially someone older than me. Thankfully, Chris really came through for me! He understood how his habits could compromise my well-being and accepted my decision to replace him. In fact, he stayed with me long enough to train my next caregiver, a nice young guy named Michael.

Michael had experience with quads and wanted a live-in position. Once he knew my routine for my care, Michael moved in as Chris moved out. Unfortunately, things with Michael took a nosedive fairly quickly. *Ugh!*

After two weeks, I became suspicious that he, also, had a drug problem. Late one night, just at the time he was supposed to get me ready for bed, he freaked out, screaming, "There are bugs all over me!" I watched as he pinched a "bug" off his clothes and then held it over a flame on the gas burner. When the "bug" shriveled in the flame, he felt confirmation that, indeed, it had been alive. Of course, since I was as sober as the day I was born, it was pretty obvious this "bug" was just a piece of lint. I tried to tell him, but he didn't believe me.

The more he freaked out, the more frightened I became. I had no experience with someone who was not sober; I had never been around anyone who was drunk or high on drugs. I had no idea what he was on or how long it would last. I was scared being around someone so unstable and unpredictable, not to mention having to rely on such a person for my health and well-being.

As I sat helplessly in my chair, I waited for two hours for him to sober up enough to help me into bed. Again, I knew I had to fire my caregiver. For the second time in a month, I had to be confrontational. Then a new fear suddenly shot into my mind. *If I fire him tonight, he could just leave. I could be stuck in bed with no one to help me if I had an emergency. And worse, who will take care of me in the morning?* For my own safety, I made the choice to wait until I found his replacement before I confronted him. I had to plan this out.

A few days later, I discovered he had been taking my ATM card and had been stealing money from my bank account to buy his drugs. Apparently, he had taken my ATM card and withdrawn twenty dollars on numerous occasions. *He absolutely has to go.* That next morning, as I sat in the shower, the hot water pouring down on me, I wanted to cry. *I know I'm helpless in so many ways, but I can't give up. I have to get through this, because if my last month is any indication of what the rest of my life might look like, I have no choice. I have to be strong.* I took a deep breath and then began quietly singing a favorite worship song from church. The lyrics described the strength God gives on a daily basis. I sang it as a prayer to God. And then I'd sing it again, replacing the word *strength* with *hope* and then *peace* and then *joy*. I felt at peace.

It would be an understatement to say that these last few months could potentially challenge my faith. So many circumstances could only be described as painful and stressful. Here I was, a young man on the threshold of the rest of my life, but I was so vulnerable. But God was faithful. He brought me such a peace in the midst of every trial and storm, just as He had always done. The Bible calls it the "peace of God which passes all understanding," as described in Philippians 4:7. It is a peace that is just unexplainable. It is amazing. It is a wonder. My heart overflowed with thankfulness. *Thank you, God!*

After two disappointing caregivers, I was also learning that hiring a stranger to be my live-in caregiver was a risky scenario. You never know what you'll get. I was discovering anyone can appear nice and polite and stable in an interview. I just prayed that God would protect me. I didn't see any other option but to try again with another live-in caregiver.

Filled with the peace that passes all understanding, when Michael went to the store, I called Bruce, a caregiver who had responded to the same ad from when I found Michael. Bruce said he could start immediately. *Good!* I phoned my aunt Cheryl to come over for moral support. As soon as she arrived, I told Michael that he had to leave immediately. He handled it well, packed up his belongings, and left just hours before Bruce moved in. *Phew! I hope Bruce isn't hiding any addictions or criminal intent.*

Bruce was tall and big and very imposing, with a big red beard to match! He was probably near fifty years old. It didn't take long for me to realize that, besides his physical appearance, there were a few odd things about him. Bruce was married but chose not to live with his wife. Also, he said that he was a narc for the U. S. Postal Service, usually helping nab bikers on drug charges. This is definitely not what most people think of when they think of a nurse/care-giver! What a relief though when I soon came to learn that, despite the oddities, Bruce was a nice guy and a reliable attendant, and the following summer, he was by my side as I returned to Grass Valley for a visit.

We came back to CSUN for my fall semester with my goal still set on earning my bachelor's degree in speech communication and becoming a high school speech teacher. The semester included the beginning of my upper division classes. Would you believe I actually enjoyed classes like Rhetorical Criticism and Persuasion? I looked forward to using information I learned in these classes with my own students someday. It was so fulfilling for me to have a direction for my life and to know that I was going to make something of my life!

Such lofty thoughts soon gave way to reality once again. In the midst of my educational momentum, Bruce announced, "I've got to leave. I've got a mission to do."

"You're joking," I responded.

"No, I'm not. I've arranged a temporary replacement to help you. She can stay until you find someone perma-nent. Her name is Maria. She doesn't speak any English." And with that, he was gone. Unbelievable.

This is exhausting.

Now what? It's hard enough to find, then train, then trust a caregiver. How do I train one to take care of me who doesn't speak English?

Maria was a cute, petite girl from Mexico. My first thought was, *Is she strong enough to lift me out of my wheelchair and in and out of bed?* I pushed that question aside for the moment and dove deep into my memory bank from my high school Spanish classes and did my best to converse with her. I was surprised by how much I remembered from high school! As we both struggled with the language barrier, we managed to communicate enough for her to learn my care. And even though she was petite, using correct body mechanics, she could pick me up!

But again, since Maria was only for the short term, with fear and trepidation, I continued my search for a live-in. I never could have predicted who that would turn out to be! My longtime friend Steve couldn't get into the college classes he needed that semester. When he heard my story and combined it with his story, he figured that God was telling him to help me out for the rest of the semester. I was thrilled! I was actually going to have a trusted and much loved friend caring for me. Granted, he had absolutely zero experience in healthcare, but he was ready, willing, and able to learn everything Maria and I taught him.

It was a little awkward to have a friend helping me with my personal care, and I'm sure the reverse was true for him. But putting embarrassment aside, he was a quick learner, and before long, he had the routine down pat.

During the day when I was in class, Steve would hang out at the dorm, exercise, and practice guitar. When I wasn't in class or doing homework, we'd watch movies, watch our favorite TV shows, listen to music, reminisce about the old days, laugh a lot, and go to church. We even went to a U2 concert for my birthday! It was so refreshing to enjoy, rather than fear, what might be coming next with my caregiver. Having a friend like Steve be so integral in my life was amazing!

With my heart full of optimism and my well-being in safe hands, I could concentrate on moving forward to become a high school teacher. I was quickly realizing that upper division classes required a lot more time if I was going to make top grades. As classes got harder and my assignments piled up, I often couldn't even begin to write my papers until one or two days before they were due. I managed to keep up somehow, but imagine if you could only type one key at a time!

Typing my papers took forever! My professors were understanding and allowed me to type in all caps because it was easier for me, but I still ended up having to pull some all-nighters. CSUN offered me typing services, but having challenged myself all my life, I wanted to be the one typing my own papers.

During those brief moments in-between assignments, I contemplated on where I would someday like to teach. There was only one answer for me—my alma mater, Nevada Union High School. I phoned Mrs. Wasley, my favorite dean from high school, and Mr. Brown, my favorite teacher. Their excitement at the idea of having me work there made me even more determined.

Because Mr. Brown was still the speech teacher at Nevada Union, I understood and accepted that, if I got hired there, I would be given English classes until such a time as he retired, and then perhaps I would be given speech classes. I was fine with that; I was just excited at the thought of being a teacher.

As the fall semester was winding down, Steve needed to leave soon and go back to Sacramento State University, and I would, once again, be looking for a new attendant. Through an ad in the newspaper, I found Bill.

Like all the others, he was a nice guy, but training him was an incredibly slow process. All my caregivers required extra time at the beginning. After all, besides learning all the different levels of care I required, caregivers also need to learn my preferences and the various routines for morning, midday, and nighttime care. But in Bill's case, well, let's just say that Bill and I had significantly opposite concepts of time.

Usually, when new caregivers learn my morning routine, it takes around three hours from the time I wake up to the time I'm showered, shaved, dressed, and ready to go. Once they got the routine down, that could all happen in two and a half hours or less. Bill, on the other hand, from the beginning, required over three hours. And for some unexplainable reason, the longer he worked for me, the longer he took. Many mornings I had to rush out the door and "floor" it to class, so I wouldn't be late.

This is when I started to realize that so many hours of my day, so much of my life, was taken up by my disability. It was not just the long morning routine, but it was also the other times throughout the day. It all added up. This was a frustrating realization. *I don't want my life to be consumed or defined by my disability. I want my life to be about my schooling, work, hobbies, relationships, and faith.* I knew my care was essential, but I wanted it minimized.

The truly best thing about Bill, though, was I could trust him. He wasn't addicted to drugs or alcohol. I couldn't envision him getting swept away in love by a woman he met. And I knew he would rather die than steal a cent from me. So in that respect, I was comfortable and content with Bill.

When summer arrived, Bill and I headed up to beautiful Grass Valley, my beloved hometown. It was great to smell the pine trees again! It was great to see my old friends and family again! My brothers had grown so much since I saw them last Christmas! It hit me how much of their lives I had missed over these last few years. As they shared about their schools, friends, and adventures, I hurt knowing I couldn't physically be there for them as a true big brother. All my time these last few years was focused on my health, attendant care, and education. I regretted having not called them more often to check in, catch up, and encourage them. They could have used a big brother's support.

I was so ready for a break from school and having an awesome summer, but reality hit when Bill started taking nearly four hours to get me ready for the day! As I analyzed why, it became apparent that he easily got unfocused on my care and that he refocused on something irrelevant. For example, one morning as Bill was about to roll me into the shower, he had noticed that the closet door was off its hinge. He started to repair the closet door and forgot all about me waiting to get into the shower. This lapse in time management happened all the time, and it was driving me nuts! He was a very nice guy, just very slow.

Because of Bill's slowness, I was unavailable to my friends and brothers in the mornings. I made up for that in the afternoon and evenings. One of the best things my friends and I did that summer was a weekly Bible study at my apartment. A few of us took turns each week as the teacher. It was a great time of fellowship, growth, and fun. And as a side benefit, I learned, firsthand, something potentially valuable if I did become a high school teacher. I learned that I absolutely had to be prepared before teaching the lesson. Being prepared meant I had to know and understand the material inside and out. I had to anticipate questions that might arise and have answers prepared. I've heard it said that the most effective way to learn is to teach, and I certainly learned the truth of that!

Then out of the blue, another totally random, unexpected, and awesome opportunity landed in my lap. I was waiting in the tire store for new tires. To pass the time, I opened a conversation with a woman seated next to me. When I asked her what she did, she shared that she worked at the local community radio station, KVMR. Since I had wanted to try DJing for some time, I took the leap and told her about my interest. To my amazement, she said she could make that happen. She put me in touch with Mike, one of the DJs, and before I knew it, he graciously offered his time slot the following Saturday for my inaugural show. Sure, it was the three dark hours between midnight and 3 a.m., but who needs sleep? I was as excited as a kid before Christmas!

Just like I prepared to lead Bible study, I got right to work on getting ready for my radio show. I dug through my stacks and stacks of CDs, picking out my favorite songs. I arranged the songs in the perfect order and typed up a playlist, noting the length of each song so that everything would fit within the timeframe of my show. I also prepared a few comedic surprises and arranged a guest DJ to join me.

About half an hour before the clock struck midnight that Saturday night, I rolled into the radio station with a bag of CDs and a smile on my face. Mike, the world's most generous DJ, greeted me in the lobby, as did my guest DJ, Mr. Brown. Mike pointed to the on-air studio, where, through the large window of glass, we could see the current DJ doing his show. *I will be at that microphone in just a few minutes!* As Mike explained some of the procedures, my mom and brothers arrived to support me and to hang out for a bit! This was going to be fun!

The current DJ started his last song and stood up, which was Mike's cue that it was our turn to enter the studio. He moved the DJ chair, so I could wheel up to the mic. Mr. Brown sat in front of the other mic, while Mike stood to monitor all the equipment. Mike took my bag of CDs and put the headphones over my ears. The CD player counted down the final minute of the last song, and I reviewed my playlist and my scripted "lines."

The song finished, Mike pointed to me, and I calmly said in my smoothest novice DJ voice, "My name is David Kline, and you are listening to KVMR 89.5." I went on to play my favorite songs, commenting on each and chit-chatting with Mr. Brown and Mike. Just to be silly, I also performed fake commercials that I had written. And since Grass Valley, being such a small town, only had a few stoplights, I just had to give a middle-of-the-night traffic update, complete with a reporter in the sky and obviously fake helicopter sound effects. Throughout the night, I took calls from listeners and let them make song requests. It was hard to believe how those three hours flew by! My time at the mic could not have been more of a thrill!

As we were leaving the building, Mike kindly offered me another gig before I left Grass Valley; I took him up on his offer. I titled my next show "David Kline's Quest for Primetime Show," and I labeled myself "The Uncola of the Airwaves" and "The Next Pet Rock."

Thanks to so many kind people, I had such a fantastic summer! And now it was time to drive south, back to LA and my senior year.

Much of that school year turned out to be fairly predictable, as I was now a "pro" at college. My exercise class was still my favorite part of the day. My upper division classes were still both interesting and difficult. My intention to keep at least a 3.5 GPA remained a top priority. Of course, church and Bible studies were up there as well. The tradition of Thanksgiving visits of my mom and my brothers still kept my spirits up for the fall semester. And to keep everything in balance, Bill was still incredibly slow. So slow, in fact, I finally couldn't take it anymore.

I finally decided that I had to let him go. Again, I hated confrontation, and Bill was such a nice guy, so it was a tough decision for me. I gently explained the situation to him; he seemed to understand why I needed to find someone else.

My next caregiver was a man from Uganda named John who was studying for his degree in civil engineering. John soon turned out to be one of my best attendants to date, but unfortunately, he could only help me until June, because his fiancé was waiting for him in Uganda, and soon he would be a husband.

Although not as exciting as marriage, I also had formed plans for June. After graduating in June, I planned to enroll at National University in Sacramento for my teaching credential. The campus was conveniently located about fifteen minutes from my mom's condo in Folsom. In addition, there were two other reasons I chose National. Each unit could be completed in one month, with classes twice a week, and I could complete my coursework in six months. So my plan was to move to my mom's home in June, start my credential program in July, begin student teaching at my alma mater in January, and then hopefully get hired there for the fall. *Wow.* I was on my way.

But first things first. Before I knew it, my four years at Northridge came to a close on a beautiful day in May, perfect for a graduation. I still couldn't quite wrap my head around the fact that it had only been about six years since my accident. I had graduated from high school and now had earned my bachelor's degree. I never doubted I could reach my goals. I never doubted God would be by my side. But, boy, was it hard work! All the struggle, all the frustrations, all the midnight marathons—in the end—paid off! I graduated with cum laude honors, as well as membership in the honor societies Phi Kappa Phi, Golden Key, and Lambda Pi Eta. I also received the Aronstem Outstanding Senior Award from the Communications Department at CSUN.

I wonder if some people, six years ago, ever thought I would be here.

On air at the KVMR studio with Mr. Brown.

With my brothers at my graduation from CSUN.

CHAPTER 13

With graduation over and CSUN, my home for the last four years, in the rearview mirror, John and I traveled back up north to my mom's. I was glad to have the opportunity to stay with her while I continued my education. Her condo was three levels, but fortunately, the bedrooms, bath, kitchen, and dining room were all on the main floor. I placed an ad in the newspaper for a caregiver and interviewed a number of applicants. The caregiver I thought was the most qualified was Amber, who, coincidentally, was cute, bubbly, and very friendly. John stayed until we had trained her, and I wished him the best in his new life and assured him that he had cared for me well. Then, as with every new caregiver adventure, I wondered how this next caregiver would turn out.

Within a couple of days, I had my answer. To start, cute Amber often seemed somewhat tipsy. Next, I discovered she was smoking in my van. When my mom and I confronted her with the evidence, I added habitual liar to the growing list of why I needed to, once again, start a new attendant search. I'd long ago learned that if attendants give themselves permission to lie to my face, they most often give themselves permission to cheat and betray me in other ways.

She also started becoming a bit flirty, but I wasn't interested in her. A few days later, she told me that she was in love with me. The next morning, while she was helping me in the shower, she suddenly said, "It's hot out," and she took off her shirt. I was shocked! *This is really awkward!* I didn't know what to do, so I just closed my eyes. Seriously. That sounds kind of funny, but there was no way I was falling for a girl with low morals who was also a liar, smoker, and an alcoholic!

I fired her the next day. I had a suspicion that there was still a piece missing to the Amber puzzle. Sure enough, after she left, we found that my mom's cooking sherry bottles, hidden high in the top kitchen cabinet, were all empty.

All I could wonder, jokingly and seriously, was, *Do girls have to get drunk to like me? I hope not.*

With no time to waste, I contacted Troy, a caregiver whom I had interviewed a week earlier. He was still available, and he was at our door within the hour. He was twenty-two years old and had long, long blond "rocker" hair. Yes, the rocker hair seemed pretty silly, but he had a good sense of humor, and we got along well. Troy not only drove me to the weekly Bible study that my friends and I had started up again in Grass Valley, he seemed to be really blessed by the study and the fellowship with my friends. In a short time, he felt like part of our family.

So with my attendant situation taken care of, I placed all my focus on the start of my teaching credential program in July. My enthusiasm diminished a bit when I learned that the state of California did not offer a teaching credential in speech communication. This did not mean that I could not teach speech; it just meant that I would have to get my credential in a different subject. So I chose English because it seemed somewhat related to speech and I had done good (I mean, *well*) in all my English classes.

This credential issue also presented another problem. Every aspiring teacher was required to pass the National Teacher Exam (NTE), an exam that tested a person's knowledge of his/her chosen subject matter. The exam was being offered in July. As I mentioned, there was no credential for speech communication and thus no NTE for speech. So with no preparatory classes and with a somewhat limited background of knowledge, I would be tested, not in my area of speech, but in English. *Well, now. That changes things. But I can handle it. I've always earned As and Bs in English.*

As I was getting settled in at my mom's, my first class at National University started. It turned out to be pretty easy. A lot of the information we covered I had already learned in college, like in my psychology class. Also, most of the work we were doing was group work. This was not bad at all. What turned out to be very difficult was the NTE. Yikes, it was tough! I was good at English, and I knew a lot about English literature, but I did not know that I needed to know *everything* about English, as in Old English, Middle English, children's literature, and on and on. *I should have researched what type of questions would be on the test!* I assumed I passed, but probably not with flying colors. Now I had to wait six weeks for the results. *Ugh!*

Meanwhile, I was cruising through my teaching credential classes. They were easy, and I was getting good grades. I was also learning some skills and information that might be useful later on, such as the various types of student learners and disciplinary techniques.

School consumed most of my focus and attention, but I managed to acquire an additional interest—motivational speaking. An educator at a local elementary school had heard about me and asked if I would share my story with the kids. The offer really excited me, as I hoped I could be an inspiration to young people. I planned to tell my story chronologically, branching off from time to time to tell jokes, side stories, and medical explanations. When I entered the school cafeteria, a couple hundred pairs of young eyes turned toward me. I was excited for this opportunity, and the principal got the kids excited too as he gave me a warm welcome. I began my speech with a joke my dad used to say, "I was born at a very young age." This brought on laughs from the students who got the joke. I was touched by how attentive every student was as I shared not just my accident and issues of disability, but my whole life story.

I then invited them to ask me questions—any questions. At first, just one hand went up. "Can you drive?" a boy asked.

"Good question!" I responded, hoping to encourage other inquisitive students. I explained that I had my license before my accident, so I knew how to drive. I also explained my experience of a couple years prior when test-driving a wheelchair-accessible van that had hand controls. The kids thought that was pretty cool.

More hands went up, and I wondered if I was going to get the "How do you go to the bathroom?" question or the "Can you have children?" question, but I think they may have been a bit too embarrassed to ask those questions.

They did ask how I type on the computer and if I sleep in my wheelchair. One little boy told a five-minute story about how his uncle is in a wheelchair, which led another student to tell us how her friend broke her arm. I just smiled. The kids were precious!

My speech went great, I'm assuming, for the children were attentive, they laughed at my jokes, asked good questions, and the staff gave me positive feedback. I enjoyed the experience so much, my mom, whose friend was an elementary school principal, arranged for my next speech. That school paid me two hundred dollars! I now had the motivational speaking bug!

My mom continued to arrange speaking engagements for me. Sometimes I was paid, sometimes not, which was fine; I wasn't doing it for the money. I spoke to kindergarteners through high schoolers. For the high schoolers, I often presented my story in gymnasiums packed with students. I never was nervous, for I knew my own story and I knew it could be inspirational. I always hoped that my message of faith and perseverance would reach a number of my audience. Of course, in a group that large, there would be many athletes. Having once been a high school athlete, I assumed these kids shared the same dreams of playing in college or the pros as I once had. As I shared my pre-accident success story, with photographs on the screen of me playing basketball, running track, and kicking goals, I could see the sadness, the confusion, the disbelief, and the "could this happen to me?" fear in their faces. Giving them the contrast between my life as an athlete and "normal" kid with my life now brought a certain reality check in knowing how fragile our lives and our futures are. I hoped and prayed that all the students could see, through my example, that life could go on through tough circumstances, which, inevitably, most of them would someday face.

Not all my moments of motivational speaking were so serious though. One of my favorite conversations happened with kindergarteners. In my attempt to explain the reality of my injury, I realized that they struggled with the fact that I could not feel my legs. In the simplest, most concrete terms, I explained that I had no feeling there. After about thirty seconds, a little girl, who was obviously struggling with all of this, asked, "Well, what if a dog bit your foot? Would you feel that?"

"No," I replied, "I wouldn't be able to feel that."

All the kids were silent for a bit, with priceless expressions on their faces as their minds tried to process this unbelievable information. Then a boy, with a strong, confident voice, asked, "Well, what if a snake bit you? You'd feel that, right?"

I could not hold back my smile as I assured him, "Nope, I wouldn't feel that either. It doesn't matter what kind of animal." The joy I felt from speaking to kids confirmed I was on the right track in becoming a teacher.

So along with DJing on my own radio show, I could also check off the challenge of motivational speaking. What would be next? Even with a serious disability, I still tried to do many things any able-bodied person could do. So why wouldn't I attempt skydiving? Seriously. Sure, many people have wondered, "Now why would anyone want to jump out of a perfectly good airplane?" That's a question I still ask myself today. As a kid, skydiving was never something I had dreamed of doing. In fact, until I was offered the opportunity, it had never even entered my mind as something I would want to do. But when my mom's neighbor, Duane, learned my twenty-fourth birthday was around the corner, he surprised me with two gift certificates for skydiving; one for me and one for Troy. To my surprise, I said, "Sure."

Why do we do these things to ourselves? Why do we not think before we speak? Yes, Duane is a good guy. But didn't he used to race cars? Didn't he used to take paying customers on his private stunt plane on flights designed to make them sick? And now I agreed to jump out of an airplane with this nut?!

Our death-defying leap was happening on Saturday, October 2 at the Lodi Parachute Center. The closer that date came, the more I tried not to think about it. Five days away. I was more apprehensive than excited, which is understandable. I mean, I'll be jumping out of a plane at 10,000 feet and free-falling for 30 seconds at 140 mph. When I woke up that Saturday morning, reality hit me square in the face. *Am I as crazy as neighbor Duane?* Silly me to worry! For praise be to God—as I'm sure it was His doing—that the approaching storm cancelled all skydiving flights for that day, and now I had one more week to worry...again. The fateful day arrived, and so did another storm. Thank you, God! *By the way,* I wondered, *are You trying to tell me something?*

Evidently not, for when the third Saturday dawned, there was not a cloud in the sky. It was a beautiful day for jumping out of a plane.

Oh no. I don't know if I can do it.

Troy claimed he was excited, but from the looks of his clenched jaw, I think he was really nervous. Who wouldn't be—unless you're crazy neighbor Duane?

Within the hour, my mom, Troy, and I arrived at the small airstrip. There were several planes parked outside large hangars. Duane welcomed us with a ridiculous grin on his face that did nothing to calm my racing heart. I was just trying not to throw up. Duane wasted no time in leading us to one of the hangars where professional skydivers were chatting while they examined their parachutes lying all over the floor. I began to realize this was for real when Duane introduced us to Jim, the skydiving instructor. Jim was a very big man—tall, wide, a big full beard, and a great smile that beamed enthusiasm and confidence. Maybe he could sense my fear, for he wasted no time assuring me and my mom that he was a seasoned jumper with over five thousand jumps.

Hmmm. Okay. That was encouraging.

I know, because I've been asked, that some people think that the skydiving company attached a parachute to my wheelchair and—push! Out I go! I can just picture the hilarious and frightening image of a wheelchair floating way up in the sky with a giant parachute above it.

But, no, that is not how it worked! Jim explained everything to me, and I was even more encouraged when he said I would be stuck like Velcro to him in a tandem jump. He then continued, "After we free-fall, I will pull the cord, our chute will open, we will float like eagles catching a wind current in midair, and then I will safely guide us to a gentle landing." Of course, he didn't mention that, in those first moments, we would be falling at (pardon the expression) break-neck speed.

While still not positive if I actually had the guts to jump, I then watched the required instructional video about skydiving safety. Now there's an oxymoron if I ever heard one.

Actually, I learned it was quite safe. I learned that there were two parachutes in each pack and also a gauge in each pack that would automatically release the parachute at a certain altitude if it had not yet been released manually.

Well now, this skydiving thing isn't sounding so bad.

Of course, I was thinking this while still on the ground.

With my training complete and our jumpsuits on, it was time to take the long, long walk to the plane. For some reason, I had envisioned a little single-engine aircraft, so when I saw that big beautiful, shiny chrome C-47 cargo plane from World War II—*wow! This is exciting! This is our plane!*

I drove my wheelchair up to the door. Well, actually, there were no doors; they had been removed for easy access, meaning...easy exit. And because the plane was so huge, the doorway was about five feet above the ground. *Hmmm.* Since I was the first quadriplegic this company had ever taken skydiving, we improvised, and Troy and a few guys lifted me out of my chair and into the plane. *Wow again! This plane is huge!* The whole inside had been gutted and was now packed with twenty-two professional skydivers, all in brightly colored jumpsuits, sitting on the floor.

My new best friend Jim followed me in and buckled, strapped, and fastened me onto his front so that my back was tight against his chest. I had no intention of going anywhere without him, so this was all good. Then, wanting me to be absolutely sure about my decision to jump, he assured me that at any time before our big jump, I could shake my head no and we would not go through with it.

Good, I still had a way out.

Our plane's engines were fired up, and a loud roar filled the air. We rolled down the runway. Through the open doorway, I could see a blurring landscape whizzing past, and then I felt us gradually rise into the air. I could see the tops of trees and then, farther in the distance, countless acres of farmland, growing different crops with different patterns and different colors receding farther and farther into the distance below us.

In large circular patterns, our plane rose on its way to an elevation of ten thousand feet. Despite the loud engines and the outside wind making its presence known, I felt surprisingly calm. In fact, the higher we flew, the more excited I became. I guess, now that I understood how safe I was jumping tandem with Jim and how safe skydiving was, my hesitancy melted away. I had confronted my fears, opening the door to a brand-new experience. I now "got" why Jim, Duane, and all the other jumpers had such huge grins, and I was grinning ear to ear with them!

Once we reached our desired elevation, it was time to jump. I prayed a quick prayer—for the millionth time. Jim, the one in whom I entrusted my life, stood up. I, of course, being strapped to him, stood up also. That, in itself, was an interesting moment for me. He walked us to the open doorway where the rush of wind hit our faces. Looking down, I could see the ground far below. The long line of cars on the highway looked like tiny ants heading toward someone's picnic. "Are you ready?" Jim yelled into my ear.

I looked back inside the plane. Twenty-two professional skydivers all had their eyes fixed on me. I gave them a smile. Instantly, they all cheered and gave me a thumbs-up. "Yes!" I yelled back to Jim. And out the plane we jumped.

The air rushed past us as we began free-falling. The air rushed so quickly, I couldn't even open my mouth to breathe. I didn't panic though. I still felt calm, but what did concern me was when Jim noticed that the "trailer shoot" was tangled. Before I even had time to comprehend the problem, he got it straightened and then pulled the rip cord.

Right as the parachute opened, we immediately jerked up as our descending speed greatly reduced. Our downward velocity suddenly slowed to a nice float, and the rest of the ride down was fairly quiet and peaceful. Feeling safe, I took the time to enjoy the view of the varied landscapes and farms below us. Directly below us though was the freeway, Highway 99. That was a little disconcerting. Adjacent to the freeway I could see the small airport and the grass field and our landing target. Jim directed our parachute easily toward the landing area, and as we approached, I saw three guys on the ground readying themselves to catch me. Our landing couldn't have been any smoother as Jim slid on his bottom for a few feet and the three guys cradled me and set me down gently onto the lawn. *What an awesome experience!*

Do I ever want to do it again? Not really. I'm good.

My mom and I with Troy in the background enam-
ored by the taste of a dollar bill.

Learning to drive on the streets of Los Angeles.

What a beautiful plane to jump out of!

My instructor Jim guiding us safely to our landing target.

CHAPTER 14

Back to reality, my NTE results arrived in the mail. I had to pass this test in order to be able to start student teaching in January. Anticipating that I would pass (I'd never failed a test before), I had already asked Mr. Brown and Mr. Blake to be my Master Teachers. They had both agreed. I opened the letter and read the results.

I failed.

Ughhh!

Okay. I have to take it again. This time I'll take it more seriously. This time I'll study.

The next scheduled exam was in three weeks. *That's not much time.* Given I was not used to failure and given my career plans were on the line, I went to the library and checked out anthologies of American and English literature. When I was in high school, I played around with a very simple computer language called Basic. To help me study for the NTE, I used Basic to create a literature quiz to help me prepare. I opened up the anthologies, and I input, one key at a time, all the major authors, works of literature, dates, and literary movements onto my computer.

Once that was done, I was ready to cram that information into my head. For example, my computer quiz might ask me, "Who wrote *Moby Dick*?" Or it might ask, "What did Herman Melville write?" And I would have to type in the correct answer. I requizzed myself a million times to make sure I memorized every fact. For those three weeks, my college classes went straight to the back burner!

Even with all my studying, surprisingly, the test seemed even harder my second time around. *Am I going to fail this again?!* I now had to wait another six weeks for the results. Since that would take me right into Christmas, I could only hope that opening that letter would be the best Christmas present I'd ever opened! Even better than the blue and gold Huffy BMX bike I got as a kid! If I passed, I would be student teaching on January 6.

That's cutting it close!

I immediately got back to my schoolwork for my credential class. Just before Christmas, I completed my first stage of the credential program. With that finished, I left my mom's condo and moved to Grass Valley. Troy moved with me; he admitted having nothing better to do. My mom was sad to see me go. She was even sad to see Troy go, for by now, she was introducing him as her "fourth son." I found an apartment near the high school, trusting that all my studying had paid off and I would soon be student teaching at my alma mater! Of course, that depended on passing the NTE, so I was doing a lot of extra praying those days!

Well, I didn't pass, and I never became a teacher. Just kidding. I passed the test and was allowed to start student teaching. *Phew!*

At 8 a.m. on January 6, Troy dropped me off for my first day back on the campus I knew so well, the campus I had experienced as a student athlete and then as a quadriplegic. Troy headed off to his college class at Sierra College, and I wheeled over toward Mr. Blake's classroom for English 1. It was passing period, so there were students everywhere! As was my custom, I smiled at every person I passed. I arrived at the classroom and asked a young man to open the door for me.

Entering into a noisy room with a number of students milling about and chatting, I scanned the room and spotted Mr. Blake at his desk. He spotted me too and rose to greet me. We chatted for a second just before the class bell rang. After he greeted his students, he introduced me to the class and explained why I was there. He had a good sense of humor, so he and I joked and bantered for a moment, which put the students—and me—at ease! He then proceeded to teach his lesson as I observed his skills and techniques as a great teacher. This "routine" happened through the rest of the day as I interned in speech classes and English classes with Mr. Brown. In between classes, my brothers checked in to see how I was doing, and at lunch, we ate together in the classroom! Knowing I'd be sharing a campus with them every day now that they were in high school seemed strange yet really great!

Right on schedule, Troy picked me up at 2:30 that afternoon. Evidently, my body and brain really felt the demands of a full schedule, because even though I rarely napped, by the time I got home, I couldn't keep my eyes open! I "passed out" from the sheer exhaustion and excitement of that first day of my new career!

For the first couple of weeks of student teaching, the duty of student teachers was only to observe. But on my third day, knowing that the students would be curious about my "situation," I asked both teachers if I could share my story. I wanted to get everything out on the table, as in answer any questions so that students wouldn't wonder anything about my disability and so that the issue of my disability would no longer be an issue. I began my speech with my not-so-original opening line, "I was born at a very young age," which brought on the usual laughs. However, I got my own chuckle when one sweet, naïve freshman whispered to her friend, "Oh, how sad." As I had become accustomed when telling my story, the students were polite and asked good questions. This was going to be a good semester!

My students seemed to accept me right away as a "normal" person, maybe even as a really cool guy who happened to be in a wheelchair. My Master Teachers must have noticed this positive rapport, for after just a week, my observing from the sidelines quickly shifted to, Mr. Kline, front and center of the classroom! All right! I was a little nervous, for I wanted to do a really good job. Thankfully, my Master Teachers had always been superb examples of high-level teaching. They started me off on small lessons, and daily I relied on their observations, experiences, and advice to teach me how to teach. Before long, I was doing all the teaching.

I found that all my time after school in the afternoons and evenings and weekends became consumed with planning lessons and grading papers. Grading papers was challenging for me, because handwriting was still difficult and very time-consuming. When writing words, I had to hold down the paper with my water bottle so that the paper wouldn't move. After writing a comment, I would then have to pick up my water bottle, set it down off the paper, move the paper, pick up my bottle, set it back down on the paper, and then write my next comment. You can see why grading was so time-consuming! I came up with a grading system for essays that alleviated this problem. Instead of tediously writing the same comments over and over and writing them on every student's paper, I made a numbered list of twenty-four comments that I would commonly write on essays. Now I only had to write a number instead of a phrase. I could write a simple number without needing my water bottle. Then when I returned the graded essays to my students, I required my students to write the corresponding comment next to each number I wrote on the essay. You see, I had learned that most students rarely read their teachers' comments, so not only was this grading system easier for me, but it also forced my students to actually look at my comments. Devious!

To be honest though, my students were great! I loved interacting with them and joking with them. For example, I developed a list of sarcastic replies for when a student would ask me, "Mr. Kline, can I go to the bathroom?" I would answer, "Well, I'm not a medical professional, so I don't feel qualified to answer that question." Or I might say, "You're fourteen years old, so I'm going to assume you've figured out how to by now."

The student would laugh and say, "Mr. Kline! *May* I go to the bathroom?"

My students were also very kind and respectful to me. They even helped me with passing out papers and writing my notes on the board for me. Whenever I asked for a volunteer, more than enough hands would go up! So far, student teaching was a fantastic and worthwhile experience.

Unfortunately, things couldn't go too well in my life for too long. I was checking my bank statements one afternoon, and something didn't seem quite right. To be specific, I was short four thousand dollars, and there were three checks I couldn't account for! As this was a private matter, I waited until Troy was out of the house before calling my bank's After Hours Automated Teller. The balance confirmed what I feared. My mind raced. Not only was I crushed that all the money I had scrimped and saved was gone, but I was also devastated and frightened by the thought that someone had actually stolen from me, maybe even someone close to me.

Who did this? My friends and family couldn't have done this. There's only one person with access to my checkbook. Troy.

I hated to think it, but he seemed to be the only culprit. What a betrayal! Not only was he my trusted caregiver, he was my friend.

Life in a wheelchair put me in a very vulnerable position. If I casually asked him about the money or straight out accused him of theft, I could trigger anger in him. He then might harm me physically and/or leave. Either way, I had no defense for my personal safety, nor did I have anyone to replace him for my personal care.

So to protect myself, I first had to get absolute proof of what seemed to be true. To keep Troy "in the dark," I had him drop me off at my dad's office the next day after school, so I could call the bank manager and discuss my suspicions. The manager confirmed that the three checks were each written to Troy. *Sigh! I have to fire him.* I arranged for the manager to send copies of the checks to my dad. It would take three long days. In the meantime, I had to pretend as though I was unaware that Troy, my trusted caregiver and friend, was, in reality, a thief and a liar.

Forefront in my mind was the reality that once I had Troy arrested, I would be without anyone to take care of my needs. The only one I could think of who might have the time and ability to help me was Bill. From my dad's office, I phoned him and explained my situation. Without any hesitation, he replied, "David, I'm ready to help you anytime."

Even though I knew Bill would soon arrive, those three days at Troy's mercy were so difficult. Can you imagine trying to just be your normal self, acting like nothing is wrong while your life is in the hands of a thief?

Behind the scenes, my dad called the police to give them a heads-up. When the checks arrived, my dad brought them over to me at my apartment while Troy was at the store. Sure enough, Troy had written each one to himself and forged my signature. I had to smile though when I noticed Troy was stupid enough to write "Troy's new car" on the memo of each check.

I guess his mom didn't buy him that red Firebird he wanted.

Now that I had the physical proof, my dad and I notified the investigator and informed him of Troy's class schedule. Next, a quick call was made to confirm with Bill that he was still available. Ever faithful, he agreed to drive up from Los Angeles first thing in the morning and meet me at my apartment after school. It would all go down tomorrow at 10:15 a.m., when Troy would be sitting down for his math class. It felt like I was starring in a police detective TV show!

When the next day arrived, I played my part. Nothing out of our ordinary routine. I woke up at 5:30 a.m., and by 8, Troy had dropped me off at school. I bid him a final good-bye. Little did he suspect how this day would turn out! It was hard for me not to think about that while teaching my first two classes!

As I watched the clock turn 10:15, I took a brief pause from my teaching and reflected on what was happening and how it would affect my life. A flood of thoughts filled my head.

You're getting arrested right now, Troy. This chapter is over. I sighed. *How could you do this to me? Now, I once again have to find a new caregiver. Dealing with caregivers who are flaky or liars or drug addicts or thieves is exhausting! Finding new caregivers is exhausting! Training new caregivers is exhausting! Problems with caregivers feels as frustrating and as difficult an issue as dealing with the fact that I am quadriplegic and can't walk. I can see how some people in my situation would want to just give up. Maybe ending it all or just moving into a nursing home and vegging for the rest of one's life would be easy options for some. But thank God I have God, and He has given me faith! Once again, I have to trust Him and keep pushing forward. He has a good track record of always getting me through every trial, just as He promised.*

My attention returned to my students, who, thankfully, hadn't noticed my mental journey and were still working on their handout.

When school was over, my dad picked me up and took me back to my apartment. And true to his word, Bill was waiting for me. Talk about grateful! He immediately got back into our routine and helped me go to the bathroom and then fixed me a snack. At four o'clock, the investigator arrived to give me the play-by-play of the day's events. He and several other officers arrested Troy about 10:20 as he was getting out of his car in the parking lot of Sierra College. Troy was a few minutes later than they had expected. Apparently, he had also gotten a speeding ticket on his way to school. *Ah, sweet justice!*

We were all having a laugh over that unexpected event when my phone rang. My dad picked up the phone, turned it on, and held it up toward my ear. I couldn't believe my ears when I heard Troy's voice! He was calling me from jail. "I'm so sorry, David," we all heard him say. "I was going to pay you back. I promise I'll pay you back. Get me outta here. I'll work extra to pay you back," he rambled on. I don't know how he could think I would ever trust him again.

"Sorry, Troy," I said and hung up.

What Troy had just handed to the investigator was his confession. He had sealed his own fate with that call. Case closed!

Wow! What a day. But I still was a student teacher, and I still had papers to grade and lessons to plan. I couldn't drop my responsibilities because of a tough day and a potentially rough future. I thanked my dad and the investigator for their help, and I got to work.

At bedtime, it felt so good to lie down after that day, and once again, I was so grateful for Bill's help. I wouldn't have been able to make it to school the next morning if it weren't for Bill (though I had to get up pretty early to be ready on time).

I rely on my caregivers so much! Yes, they help me be able to live. But if they are slackers or are late, I won't make it to school. I'd be out of a job (student teaching doesn't pay, but you get the idea). I have to have responsible caregivers. Everything has to be seamless.

As Bill could only help out for a short amount of time, once again I was on the hunt for my next caregiver. I placed an ad in the newspaper and waited for the phone to ring. But miracle of miracles, before I even interviewed any applicants, my high school friend Darren heard about my recent struggles and offered to help. Even though he'd never been a caregiver before and I would need to train him, I was so relieved! Helping someone with bathroom care, bathing, and dressing was a completely new experience for him, and it proved to be a challenge for him. But what a trooper and a good friend, for he hung in there and learned my care. When he was trained and ready to take over, it was time to say a very sincere thank-you to Bill. He definitely was a godsend!

The months seemed to fly by, probably because I was busy with student teaching, finishing up a few more credential classes, and accepting invitations for motivational speaking. It felt great to be in the "zone," knowing all of it was bringing my goal closer to reality. And then I got the call I had forgotten was coming.

The investigator had a bit of a surprise regarding the outcome of Troy's trial. Obviously, he was found guilty. His car would be sold, and I would be repaid the money he had stolen. But no way was I prepared for what came next. I learned that this was Troy's third felony! A few years before, he had been convicted for car theft and child endangerment. California's Third Strike law meant that he would be going to prison, and he was sentenced specifically to Folsom Prison. *That is serious!*

I bet your fellow inmates will love your pretty, long, blond hair, Troy.

Okay, back to reality. My semester of student teaching was coming to a close, and I reflected on all I had learned. I had quickly realized that teaching in a classroom was a whole different ballgame than learning theories of teaching in a credential class. My Master Teachers had taught class management, such as how to discipline students and deter potentially disruptive behaviors. I learned that teaching is incredibly time-consuming. Most of all, I learned that high school students are great. They can be challenging and frustrating at times, but overall, they're nice, fun, good kids. I would miss this group of students.

CHAPTER 15

That summer, while waiting for my teaching credential, I received a very unexpected offer. I was out with friends at a local concert one evening when a man came over to me and introduced himself as Bob Britts. "I've heard a lot about you," he said. "You were a great soccer player in your day. Would you be interested in coaching my son's soccer team?"

Wait! What? Wow! A flood of thoughts instantly rushed into my brain! *I can do this. My wheelchair can go over grass just fine. I have eleven seasons of soccer experience still in my brain. I'd love to be involved in the great game of soccer again!* "What age group is the team?" I asked.

"Twelve and thirteen years old. They're in junior high. It's a club team."

I wouldn't want to coach really young players, players with very few skills, but junior high–aged players would be fine. They would have skills that I could work with and develop. "Yeah, I'll do it," I said with a smile. *This is awesome!* I was so excited.

"Fantastic!" Bob said. "My son Austin will be so happy!" Bob gave me his phone number and then, thinking ahead, offered to drive me in my van to and from each practice.

The next morning, I got right to work preparing for my first practice, as I had spent most of the night lying awake reviewing drills and exercises in my head. Most of my ideas I drew from my experience as a player, specifically under the excellent coaching of Thad Kopec at Forest Lake Christian School. He had made sure we were in good shape, had good ball control, and were skilled in the foundations and basics of soccer. I liked that. I agreed with that. I would train my players like that. I sketched out drills in an ordered list for my first practice. I planned the specific time required for each drill. I even called Coach Kopec to ask him for any new drills he was using. He was so thrilled to hear that I was making a return to the soccer field!

When Bob and I drove up early to practice, his son Austin was already on the field kicking a ball with a few other players. I met Austin and the others while more players showed up. Once everyone arrived, I had my players sit on the grass in front of me. Even though I was pretty sure Austin knew of my reputation with a soccer ball and had likely told others about me, I still wanted to share an official introduction and brief explanation of who I was. I told them all about my soccer experience and success, and I told them a little about my accident. Then it was time for practice!

To establish our routine right up front, I had my players jog and then sit in a circle for their stretches. I talked them through all the stretches I wanted them to do each practice. As they stretched, I used the time for them to introduce themselves. It turned out they all had known each other for years! Once the "formalities" were out of the way, the boys started chit-chatting, and I could see their personalities coming through. I had to smile. Before me stretched a truly funny, sweet bunch of kids! And they were my team!

I then explained our first drill and split them into groups. We continued through the practice, working through the drills I had planned. When a drill required demonstration or further explanation, I had Austin and a couple other boys demonstrate it. All the players were attentive and respectful to me, and they worked very hard. Not one of them ever gave me the impression that because their coach was physically limited, they were cheated out of having a good coach. If that first day was any indication, we were going to have a great time that season! Not to mention how thrilled I was to be back on the soccer field after seven years! I could feel the excitement in my bones! Coaching was bringing a whole new joy to my life!

Thank God, because becoming gainfully employed as a teacher was proving to be a bit challenging! My high school wasn't hiring new teachers that year, so I pursued substitute teaching until they were. Working as a sub would at least get my foot in the door for the next year. That is, if my credential managed to get past some paperwork complications from my university. Every time I called to find out what the problem was, the only answer was, "It should be taken care of soon." *Hmmm.*

At least I had my soccer team, now officially called the Rattlesnakes, a name that sounds very threatening. For weeks, these kids had given their all at every practice! We felt prepared and ready for our first game! We were the away team, travelling about thirty minutes to meet our opponents. Once there, my players got their cleats on and started their synchronized warm-up. The synchronized warm-up was my players' idea, but I had to admit, it did make them look disciplined, focused, and intimidating. I then had the boys huddle around me, and I said a quick prayer. I had previously designated the starters and team captains for the game, and when it was time, they took to the field. Not even ten minutes into the game, Andrew, our center forward, got the ball, outran our opponent's defense, and scored. It was great! Not long after, he did it again. And then again. The entire team played fantastic that day. We won 7-0! I was thrilled. The players were thrilled. The parents were thrilled.

A number of things were going on as the school year started. First of all, my friend and current caregiver, Darren, made the choice to move to southern California to continue college. His help, when I had needed it most, was a true gift at the perfect time, and now he needed to move on in his life. While I was extremely grateful, I was also very frustrated with my recurring dilemma.

Can I just have a caregiver last longer than a few months?! If it's not them moving away, it's me having to fire them!

My next caregiver ad in the newspaper yielded Karen. She was a musician who had some caregiving experience. She was also quiet and mellow, which I appreciated in a live-in caregiver.

The other major issue that fall was that my university was still trying to finalize my credential, so unfortunately, I could not yet be hired as a substitute teacher. National University informed me they still needed more paperwork, which they then would submit to the state. *Ugh!*

The highlight of my days was my Rattlesnakes! Those up-and-coming athletes were winning most of our games! I was having a blast with those kids! They were such good boys and so funny! Their parents were great too and were very supportive of the team and of me. By the end of the season, we only lost to one team and ended up in second place in the league. Not bad for my first year of coaching! We had grown so close as a team that none of us were ready to "let go." So I continued to coach them after the season was over in an indoor soccer league. For each game, a parent loaded me and some players into my van and drove us thirty minutes to the game. Our team really felt like a family.

Finally, my teaching credential came through. *Yay!* I was so close to achieving my goal! Unfortunately, because of the delay in my paperwork, I had missed out on an entire semester of substitute teaching. I was ready now. The tough thing for me about subbing though was that substitutes receive a phone call between 6-6:30 in the morning and then have to be at school by 7:20. If I got a call at 6 and started getting up at that time, I wouldn't be ready until around 8:30 a.m. This was a problem. I couldn't be available on-call like most subs. Fortunately, I was close to a handful of teachers, including Mr. Brown and Mr. Blake, so they agreed to let me know ahead of time what day they needed me. On those days, I got up extra early in the morning to be at school on time.

Believe it or not, I never had any horror stories while subbing like those poor substitute teachers in movies and TV shows. Maybe it was the wheelchair that struck the students out of the blue, or maybe it was that I really focused on keeping the kids on task while also joking around with them. I do know that several students I had taught the previous year had shared with friends that "Mr. Kline is pretty cool." For whatever the reasons, the students really made my time as a substitute teacher enjoyable.

Subbing was fine and all, but it was not my goal. My goal for years had been to teach my own students. I wanted my own classes. I wanted my own room. I got a step closer to that goal when an English teacher announced that she was retiring at the end of the year, meaning there would be an opening for the next school year that fall. I put my application in immediately! There was more good news at the school. Nevada Union was looking to hire a new Junior Varsity soccer coach. I applied for that too. This was all looking too perfect.

Could I get both dream jobs?

Since the interview for the English position would take place during the middle of the summer, I first interviewed for the coaching job. I brought with me letters from my players and parents, all lavishing praise on my job as their coach. During the interview, I answered the athletic director's questions and shared my background and my philosophy on coaching. I'm sure he had never imagined that he would be interviewing someone in a wheelchair to coach a soccer team, but I was not deterred. I felt confident that with my history, expertise, and last season's success, I was a good candidate. Plus, most of my Rattlesnakes would be moving up to the JV team that year. Truth be told, I so loved those kids that being able to coach them for at least another season was the real reason I wanted the coaching position. I wanted to continue to support them in their progress of becoming the best players and young men they could be. A few days later, I got the call from the athletic director. I got the job! I was now the JV Boys Soccer Coach! *Awesome!*

With tryouts starting in one week, I faced a new reality. When I had coached the Rattlesnakes, I didn't have to cut any players. Now, with so many new kids trying out, I knew "cutting" players was going to hurt the kids...and me.

When we met for the first time on the field that summer, I hugged all my former players and met all the new kids. Then, like I did the previous year, I sat them down and told them my story. Then we got to work.

My former players were excited to tell me about a particular player trying out who they thought was really good, but after a week of practice, I wasn't impressed with him. There was talent there, but he showed no interest in working hard or proving to me that he should make the team. When it was time for me to make cuts, as hard as it was for me, I cut him. Not only some of my kids, but their parents too, told me they were surprised by my choice. But once I explained my rationale, they agreed with my judgment. For the record, during try-outs the next year, he worked *very* hard, demonstrating that he was committed to earn his place on the team. All part of my plan. He was a great kid and proved himself to be one of our best players.

Our practices were going great out there that summer. The smell of fresh cut grass still drew me to the soccer field! I didn't care for the heat though. Boy, it was hot! My mornings though were spent in a nice, cool, air-conditioned classroom as I taught summer school four days a week.

On less typical days, I organized playlists and CDs in preparation for my occasional midnight gig as DJ of the "David Kline Quest for Primetime" radio show. I also was hired as a motivational speaker at several high schools. I guess I did a pretty good job, because one of the school principals, a professional speaker herself, noticed the impact I had on her students and suggested I consider a full-time career as a motivational speaker. That was a nice vote of confidence! I had heard that professional speakers could make a lot of money, much more than a high school teacher! I started to toss the idea around in my head. It was very tempting to consider a career in speaking. I could decide my own schedule. I could travel outside of my own small town. Most importantly, my story could potentially inspire more people as a motivational speaker. Yet I had given my all for many years to someday teach high school, and I was on the cusp of teaching and coaching at my beloved alma mater. My decision would carry profound consequences for my life. I knew God would give me clarity if I asked Him. I stopped what I was doing at that very moment and silently prayed, *Dear God, please give me wisdom. Please give me direction. Open the doors and make it clear where You want me to go. Thank you. In Jesus' name, Amen.*

Within days, my high school officially listed the English position. Nevada Union was a great high school, surrounded by towering pines and in a very desirable, historic community. So along with a mere one hundred other hopeful teachers, I submitted my application. I clung to the three advantages that I possessed that most of the other applicants did not. No, not a spinal cord injury! Nevada Union often chose to hire its alumni. NU also liked to hire teachers who could coach. Plus, my commitment to teaching at a high level was evident as a student teacher, substitute teacher, and summer school teacher. These were all items in my favor!

The hiring committee at the high school evaluated the applications, and I was selected among a handful to interview. As was my habit and as I did before my coaching interview, I prepared. I created a sample lesson plan. I compiled a stack of letters of recommendation from parents, teachers, and principals. I prepared answers to potential interview questions. And I picked out a blue and gold tie, NU's school colors.

On that pivotal day, I rolled into the principal's office for my interview. *This is the moment I had been anticipating for many years!* Sitting around a large table was the principal, the vice principal, a dean, the head of the English department, and another teacher. I had met each of them before, and they all greeted me with a smile and a warm hello. My nerves took a backseat, knowing I was well prepared. I handed them my paperwork, and then they began their questions. What was my understanding of lesson plans and instruction? How would I handle classroom disruptions and discipline? What had I learned from my experience as a student teacher? There was an ease to my answers and an obvious rapport in the room. As I left the interview, they wished me well and promised that I'd know their answer within the week. I breathed a sigh of relief, confident in my interview, but unsure how it would all turn out.

I do want this job. I hope I get it. I have worked so hard to get this far. It's all up to God now.

Waiting that week for an answer was torture! Summer school was over, but I still had soccer practice to keep my mind occupied. I knew that I had friends and family praying for me that week. I was even aware that they had been praying for me for years. I was nervous, yet calm. I knew that God was in control. I knew that He would put me wherever He wanted to use me, and I went right back to my favorite promise in the Bible, Romans 8:28, which states, "God causes all things to work together for good to those who love God, to those who are called according to His purpose." *It'll all work out!*

I finally received the phone call. "David, would you like to teach English at NU?"

I was thrilled. "You bet!" I said.

Phew! Wow! I made it! Praise God!

My team!

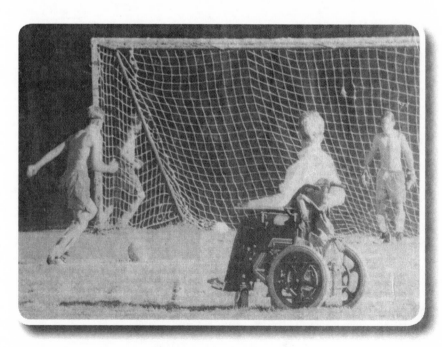

Soccer practice with my boys.

CONCLUSION

What a mountain I had to climb, with so many valleys on the way. Who would've thought, when I was nearly dying in that intensive care room with a fresh spinal cord injury eight years ago, that, not only would I be alive and well, but that I would be teaching English and coaching soccer at my old high school! It's gotta be God! There's no way I could have gotten through this without Him!

I can see that through all the hard times, all the struggles, all the trials, God was always right there with me and got me through each one. And I can see how He sprinkled little blessings along my difficult journey. And I can say that God is good when things are good and God is good when things are bad.

God doesn't change. He is always good. Sometimes it's just difficult to see that while in the midst of a trial. Somewhere along my journey, I came across an encouraging way to look at life. It's a view that puts everything into perspective. It's an analogy that compares our lives to a parade. We are standing (or sitting) on the sidewalk,

225

watching life events go by like floats at a parade. We can see the float right in front of us just as we can see today's events in our lives. We can look back at our lives at the floats that have already gone by. We can discuss our past in terms of good or bad. We can also try to get a glimpse of what is to come next in our lives, peeking down the street for the next float. We can make plans for our future, but we don't know if they will come to pass. We really have no idea of exactly what is coming. A bad or boring past doesn't mean that the floats or events to come will be the same. Maybe the best is yet to come...maybe just around the corner...maybe just a few blocks away. Who knows? But what hope we can have! We can look at our future with the same anticipation as a spectator at a parade. There are so many wonderful possibilities for each of us! And God is up in heaven looking down over the parade, over our lives, and can see the entire thing. He sees the Big Picture. We can take comfort in knowing that He can see the beginning and the end. He knows what blessings are just around the corner for us. And He's whispering, "Just hold on. Be patient. Trust Me." I love that analogy!

I've relied heavily on the fact God sees and knows everything. He knows the desires of my heart. He knows that I haven't been healed like I had hoped I would. He knows if I'll be healed tomorrow, in ten years, or not until heaven. I have come to accept that. As much as I would love to be healed right now, I know that God sees the big picture and that His timing and His plans are best. I guess that's where faith comes in.

My aunt Cheryl loved to knit cross-stitch patterns. She made designs of animals and rainbows and things like that, and she gave them away as gifts. Sometime after my accident, she gave me a cross-stitch with no design or picture on it, just a simple phrase. It came in a nice wooden frame, and I placed it above the door in my living room. It read, "We are all faced with a series of great opportunities brilliantly disguised as impossible situations."

Many people have told me that they would not be able to handle or survive being a quadriplegic. It's understandable that many would think that my life, a life without the use of my legs or hands and dependent on others, is an impossible situation. But I do not see it that way. I believe in a big God. With God, there are no impossible situations, only great opportunities. To me, this disability is a great opportunity. God is using me to accomplish things I never would have even thought of before my injury, and He is using me to reach people I most likely would not have been able to had I not had this injury. God has given me the opportunity to trust Him, praise Him, and point others to Him. I am confident that if I keep my eyes on Him, say what He wants me to say, do what He wants me to do, He can take me anywhere. With God, all things are possible.

Someone once told me his theory on why this diving accident happened to me. He believed, like I did, that my accident happened for a reason. But he took this a step further. He wondered if my accident was intended to happen, that it was part of an intentional plan. He proposed the idea that God needed someone to be able to minister to a particular person in a particular way, and so He chose me for the job. God knew that a particular person would need to hear about Jesus and that that person would only listen to someone like me in the physical condition I was in. That's quite a theory. When I first heard it, I thought it could be true. Today, I still think it could be true. I guess

I should be honored to be used by God. And in the big picture, if one person would come to Jesus because of the faith, hope, and attitude that I maintain, this disability, and all its challenges, would all be worth it. Someone's eternity is more important than a handful of decades on this planet. That actually gives me hope. It gives me joy.

God Bless!

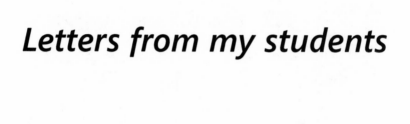

Letters from my students

Mr. Kline,

Thank you so so so much for everything you have done for me this year! You are an amazing teacher and person! I feel so blessed to have met you! You really are a huge inspiration in my life! You've gone out of your way numbers of times this year for me, and I thank you so much for that!! I do believe teachers now just don't care......you are the exception. I believe you care so much for all of us! And it shows and really means a lot to all of us. I just feel like God blessed all of us by sending you to us! Honestly. I hope God keeps blessing you like He has blessed me. Thank you for making freshman year so much easier and funner (Ha! :)) for me.

Love,
Lindsay G.

P.S. – Thanks for being the real thing.

Dear Mr. Kline,

I am not writing to give my ideas on how the class could be improved, because I do not think I would write a single word. I just want to thank you for an outstanding year of English. Day in and day out, you proved to me that you were an excellent teacher and a great person. Whether it was taking the whole class on a wonderful field trip, or having us write about our new classmates, you strove to bring the whole class, including yourself, into a nice sixth period family. When it was time to get serious with English work, you were the best at teaching us what we had to know. At times, I felt a little overwhelmed, but I kept telling myself that all the hard work was your righteous way of preparing us for the near and far future. But you did not limit yourself to just preparing us for English, for you also took time to prepare us for life. You told us how we could succeed and you told us how it would be easy to take the road to a dark future and that we should stay away from that path. And lastly, there was the humor that you brought into each day. It lifted my spirits and put the cherry on top of an already enjoyable class. I will miss you and will be forever grateful for the memorable journey that my schedule plainly called English 1 taught by Mr. Kline, but was clearly so much more.

Sincerely,
Josiah B.

P.S. – Go Cowboys!

Dear David Kline,

Hey Mr. Kline! Before I leave Nevada Union, I would like to tell you how much of an impact you were on me throughout my years here. We first met my junior year when I had you as my teacher for English 3. I enjoyed the way you taught and the connection you built with me and the entire class. I then became your Teacher Assistant my junior year which was great because I got to see you two times a day! As senior year came around I knew that I just had to be associated with you again. I had a TA position in my schedule, and the first teacher I thought of being a TA for was you. These last two years of high school have been great mainly because you were there. When I begin my own life after high school, I am still going to use the things you taught me. I plan to become a teacher as I grow into an adult and I wanted you to know that you are a big part of that decision. You also showed me that if there are bumpy roads in life, you just have to believe, which is what exactly what you did. I will be back in the later years to say hey and see how you are doing. I just wanted you to know how much of an impact you were on me and that you will have many other kids that you will impact just like me.

Sincerely,
Blake S.

Dear Mr. Kline,

I wanted to take a moment and let you know that my husband and I are praying for you. On the first day of school our son Jeff came home telling us about his teachers. He said he was certain that you were a Christian. I was so excited! We pray that God would infiltrate Jeff's life in every way possible.

He shared with us how you became disabled. What a story. We wept as we heard your reaction and how you were still within your mind. I must say, I felt encouraged to hear of your faith in our Awesome God! What assurance to all who heard that there is certainly a God who has a plan for us.

Please know that we are praying for you. May this be a year where God uses you mightily in the lives of your students! Again, thank you for your boldness with those students.

All our gratitude and admiration to you, Mr. Kline!
Margaret and John S.

Dear Mr. Kline,

I must admit that upon entering Speech & Debate on the first day I was a tad disinclined about it. It was a major change going from A.P. Biology first period to S&D second, if you know what I mean. I only knew a couple of students to top off my reluctancy. Yet as the school year progressed I came to appreciate the class more and more. I remember sitting in class in the first few weeks of school and reading all the messages from students on your classroom wall illustrating how wonderful you are and thinking to myself "C'mon, this man cannot be worth all of this hype." But at the same time I thought "Now watch, I am going to be on the same boat eventually." And here I am.

You, Mr. Kline, are truly a one of a kind teacher. You are sincere and sympathetic. You are intelligent and witty which makes you humorous while you balance it with seriousness. You are an overall beautiful person. And for this I thank you so much.

Earlier you asked if anyone would be able to give you any information on how the class was and how you could possibly enhance it. Unfortunately, yet fortunately, I have none. I truly think that you did an impeccable job teaching us.

Once again, thank you Mr. Kline for all that you have done, and I wish you all the best.

Sincerely,
John S.

Dear Mr. Kline,

Please forgive the lack of creativity in my introduction. I'd like to get right into the sappy emotional stuff. Before I met you Mr. Kline, I didn't think of myself as one of the lucky girls to have someone in their life they considered a father, born having one or acquired one over time. You have been the closest thing to a dad I've ever known. I can never return that feeling because I can't even put my emotions into words when it comes to what you have made me feel. I suppose a start would be the word complete. You never fail to make me smile and allow me to dump last night's torment whenever I need to. You're always there and that's something I've never had. You are an amazing person. I'm pretty sure you know this but you have touched the lives of so many students and I'm one of the lucky students who has had you as a teacher. The memories I made in Speech & Debate are ones I'll cherish forever. Before I had signed up to take the class, speaking in front of people was extremely difficult for me. Your class allowed me to spread my wings and figure out what works for me.

This is not goodbye. I will visit you frequently and you will stay in my life forever. Your smile fills my heart, your jokes fill my head with confused laughter, and your positivity fills your classroom. I'll miss you and your class but never forget. Thank you for being you.

Love,
Madison C.

ABOUT THE AUTHOR

David taught English and Speech/Debate for seventeen years at Nevada Union High School in Grass Valley,
California. He also coached the JV Boys Soccer team for
four years, earning the school's only undefeated soccer
season in school history. In addition to his work at the
high school, David has acted, disc-jockeyed, skydived, and
shared his story with thousands of adults and children.

CPSIA information can be obtained
at www.ICGtesting.com
Printed in the USA
LVOW11*1215140517
534485LV00001B/25/P